'Bruce has written this wonderful book which is filled with his personal experience, insights and wisdom. Readers will find strategies to help them manoeuvre the work space and make the most of their work journey, whatever that may entail. This book is engaging, clear, and full of wise, practical recommendations.'

Dr Despina Sfakinos – co-founder of MAD Psychology

'Over the past 30 years, Bruce has gained valuable experiences and insights from working across multiple industries, in multiple geographies. Sharing and combining these with his proactive, practical outlook makes this book a great resource – for those starting out or starting anew.'

Andrew Caminschi – Senior Advisor at JB North & Co

'Bruce has a very strategic approach to Human Resources and People Management, with both business and employee growth and development in mind.'

Michael Montelioni – Business and Hotel Services Manager, Whiddon Group.

'Don't have a mentor? That's okay, this book will be yours!'

Ilona Charykova – Social Media Executive, Crown Melbourne

'The book is a truly empowering read and an excellent guide on self-management. It can serve as both a coaching framework for aspiring professionals who want to take control of their careers and a statement on the future of work.'

Ludmila Hyman, Culture Strategist and Change Facilitator. Carnegie Mellon University.

Performance Matters

The ultimate career survival guide

Bruce Harkness

Published in Australia in 2018 by Bruce Harkness

Email: bruce.harkness@gmail.com
Website: www.bruce-harkness.com

ISBN 9780648144809 (paperback)

NATIONAL LIBRARY OF AUSTRALIA

A catalogue record for this book is available from the National Library of Australia

Disclaimer

The author has made every effort to ensure the accuracy of the information within this book was correct at the time of publication. The author does not assume and hereby disclaims any liability to any party for any loss, damage or disruption caused by errors or omissions, whether such errors or omissions result from accident, negligence, or any other cause.

Contents

Foreword

Love or loathe the term, 'Millennials' (those born between 1982 – 2004) are the future workforce. But the current working environment is in a state of flux, careening between a more traditional organisational culture and values, and new economies, increasing technology, and the growing demands of a generation that expects more from their workplace.

This is the environment that I stepped into as a new graduate and, most recently, as a 'Millennial' first-time manager. All of a sudden, I was navigating a corporate world at a senior level. There were expectations thrust upon me (admittedly, the majority were my own). I had to make difficult decisions. Harder to reconcile was that my career success no longer hinged in whole on my direct actions, but rather on the actions of my new team. A team I had to coach and develop.

Around the same time, I was lucky enough to be selected for my company's mentoring program, and was paired with a mentor; Bruce Harkness.

Bruce's career spans decades, working for some of the biggest corporations around the globe (Wyndham Worldwide, Carlson Rezidor Hotel Group, and Movenpick Hotels & Resorts, to name a few). As a human resource executive, Bruce has dedicated his life to helping develop his employees, believing that it is only through this work that he can grow himself.

I'd like to say that his advice throughout the mentorship was invaluable, but the truth was that Bruce doesn't dispense advice: he asks the right questions.

Questions that got me thinking, exploring different perspectives, and that eventually helped me hit on the right action to take. Needless to say, this taught me far quicker and far more about leadership and performance, than if I'd simply followed a set of instructions.

Overall, this is what *Performance Matters: the ultimate career survival guide* is about. Bruce takes you on a mentoring journey and equips you with the right tools, and asks the right questions, to get you where you want to be.

The development of a career vision is a key driver in giving you direction in your career. When connected with measurable goals and actions that can be linked to your career vision, this strategy will continue to guide you on your journey through the inevitable highs and lows of your career.

Looking back to the beginning of my year-long mentorship with Bruce today, I have come so far. I have a new goal that I am working towards, and enough self-awareness and development tools to approach challenges and opportunities with confidence.

Performance Matters codifies the unwritten rules of exceptional performance in the corporate world, and while it is a powerful book for those like me who are starting out in their career; it will resonate with anyone who is keen to be *more*.

Don't have a mentor? That's okay, this book will be yours!

Ilona Charykova
Social Media Executive, Crown Melbourne
October 2017

Acknowledgements

To those people who believed in me and took time to guide me and offer an opportunity when I needed it most, I am, and will always be, eternally grateful.

Mrs Young (my primary school teacher), who recognised more than a disruptive child in me.

Brian Mackie (Shihan and Seventh Dan Black Belt and principal of the Karate Academy of Japan in Western Australia), who taught me the virtue of self-discipline.

Murray Hamilton (UIAGM and IFMGA mountain guide) for his purist approach to mountain climbing; always a great metaphor for life's journey.

Douglas Maclagan (Rights4Children) for his inspiration and selfless care of others, and the valuable lesson that life is about what you give rather than what you take.

Michelle Roesler for her insight and gentle reminder that everything was okay when I most needed it.

Despina Sfakinos for creating the space to allow me to think and gain clarity during the time it took me to write this book.

Barry Robinson for his drive, enthusiasm, passion for life and the opportunity to turn concept into reality.

Finally, to Kiralee, Morgan and Sheridan, who have supported me throughout the good times and bad – family, first, last and always.

There are many, many others who have encouraged me to aspire for more and to pursue my full potential at all cost. To those individuals and the many chance encounters I have had along the way which have prompted me to reflect or to dare to take a risk and ultimately strive to be a better version of myself – I sincerely thank you all.

Introduction

Let's face it, life is competitive and on occasion, stressful and unpredictable ... and the workplace is no different!

Your career journey can change at a moment's notice, as a result of everything from a disagreement with your manager, company's restructuring or stock market jitters due to political upheaval, catastrophic weather events, acts of extreme terrorism. The list goes on. Get the picture: it's a volatile world in which we live.

With this volatility in mind, the deeper purpose of this book is to explore a range of ideas and concepts, and provide the opportunity for reflection not only to increase your chances of career survival and success but also to help you to take one step closer to realising your full potential. In addition, I hope that this book will create awareness of the importance of building an authentic and powerful personal brand that will further optimise your chances of success, higher levels of performance and satisfaction in your work regardless of what stage you are in your career life cycle.

The mantra is simple: perhaps now more than ever within the context of business it has never been more important to be adaptable and resilient. A play on

Darwin's Theory of Evolution granted but relevant all the same. Ultimately, all species need to adapt or run the risk of eventual extinction and, for you, today's working environment is no different. In an age where the customer rules and the philosophy of more for less reigns supreme, the rule book has changed; in fact, it has been totally re-written.

I consider myself to be very fortunate in that I have had and continue to have the privilege of working with some of the most amazing, inspirational and talented people I could ever hope to meet. I have observed at some length and detail how they approach their work and how they manage their careers. Through this process of observation I have identified a number of behaviours and practices that have allowed these individuals to excel at the highest levels. In the pages that follow, you will have the opportunity to understand just how these high performers managed to succeed and continually raise the bar to higher levels of performance.

You will also have the opportunity to consider and explore a range of ideas, concepts and reflect upon questions derived from both research and personal experience over the past 20 years as a result of working with a number of international organisations and their senior leadership teams within the area of change management, talent and leadership development.

My passion has always been and remains helping others to realise their potential. In doing so I have endeavoured wherever possible to assist organisations to build performance-focused cultures that develop, celebrate and reward excellence. It is my hope that in the pages that follow you will obtain some new insights with regard to how you can enhance your chances of career satisfaction and success.

This book is intended to help you to create your own definition of success, including crafting a compelling and engaging career vision, and defining and shaping your personal brand. In addition, it explores how to make fundamental change last and to develop a better understanding of how to navigate change in uncertain times.

It is dedicated to the current and future knowledge workers aspiring to find their way and make a difference in their working life. This book is also intended to provide you with some understanding of the complexity and dynamics in play within today's organisations. Most importantly, it is my hope that in some way it may help you to unleash your true potential.

Regardless of whether you are at the top of your game and want to move on to your next opportunity or you are just starting out in your career and feel you would benefit from some help, if you have a desire to perform at your best and have a satisfying career, I invite you to read on.

Chapter One

The meaning of work

We have moved beyond the age of work life balance to a place in time where our work and life have fused into one.

W hat is work and how do we define it? Is it a necessity of life or a wonderful opportunity to contribute to something bigger than yourself? The Mirriam–Webster dictionary definition of the word is as follows: 'Work is a job or activity that you do regularly in order to earn money. The place where you do your job and the things you do especially as the part of your job'. So it's apparent that the concept of 'work' is not particularly inspiring by definition. It's how you approach your work and view your work that makes all the difference. Let's now bypass the definition and move on to the meaning of work.

As the Baby Boomers fade into the twilight of their retirement years, Generation X will assume power, positions of leadership and influence. They will lead the workforce and their companies will have staff who consist of Millennials. As this new generation assumes power, they will experience very different challenges in terms of leading their companies than previous generations. Their employees will want to be inspired by leaders who are sincerely interested in their growth and development. They will expect and enjoy change, projects and technology. The lines between work and play will become even more blurred and the workplace will become a social meeting point where diversity is celebrated and innovation is the new battle cry.

The primary focus of any company whether big or small is to make a profit and the goal of any economy, regardless of its political philosophy, is growth.

Profit and growth drive business and the global economy. Like it or not, as an employee your role is to contribute to the profitability and growth of the company you work for; in other words, to add value. From an outsider's perspective, this may seem to be a very superficial reason for work but profit allows companies to expand, create jobs and provide opportunities for career progression. A flourishing economy provides the opportunity for communities to prosper and, potentially, to enjoy a better standard of living if managed correctly. This, in turn, can have a positive impact on future generations.

Nevertheless, profit and growth alone will not motivate or keep you satisfied in your job in the long term. It is the opportunity to be part of something bigger than yourself, to learn and make a meaningful contribution that will ultimately engage you in your work. For the vast majority of people, work is a necessity and the time involved in commuting to work, thinking about work and actually working takes up most of their waking hours and life. So it could be argued that it is in your best interest to find work that is meaningful and that allows you to grow and ultimately make a contribution.

The motivation to work varies from one person to the next, such as the need to pay the bills, to make a contribution, to achieve success, or because you have to or it is expected of you. For most of the working population, work is an economic necessity. As a result, work can be perceived as being repetitive and, for some, tedious and tiresome. All this sounds quite negative but I believe perspective is how you view life. Is it an un-scalable mountain or an opportunity to climb to a place unknown? Your mindset defines so much of how you view life and the same can be said for your perspective on work.

Much has been written about the importance of work and its subsequent impact on human psychology, including self-esteem and identity. At an individual level, your work shapes your perception of who you are and your level of self-esteem resulting from your perceptions of what you do. For example, 'I am just a manager in an office' versus 'I work and manage a team that produces life-saving medical equipment'.

The previous example reminds me of a story I was once told. I don't know how true it actually is but it certainly illustrates my point. A visiting dignitary approached two cleaners at NASA and asked the first cleaner, 'What is it that you do here?'. 'I just clean the floors', the first cleaner replied. When the second cleaner was asked the same question, their reply was very different: 'I help put humankind into space'. Two very different perspectives shaped by how these individuals viewed their job and the organisation they worked for.

Within a social setting, often the 'go-to' question of 'What do you do?' is a defining moment in any first-time conversation. How you are perceived is based on what the individual who asks the question truly values to be important for a career or job choice. 'Oh really, a doctor! You must be very clever'. In contrast, their internal thought could be, *She must be loaded.* 'An artist, how fascinating!

You must be very creative'. In contrast, their internal thought might be, *I thought he seemed weird*. Joking aside, and I have made some big assumptions here, what you do for work has the potential to shape how you define your own identity, place in society and how others view you. What is important is that what you do for work has meaning for you and you value it, enjoy it and can see the potential for making a contribution to something bigger than yourself.

The greatest risk to human potential is to stop dreaming of what is possible.

Within the animal kingdom, survival of the fittest and the ability to adapt to environmental change are two very strong predictors which ultimately determine a species' ability to survive into the future. From a workplace perspective, this can also be perceived as true, with survival of the fittest being replaced by the ability to add value and to be relevant as being of paramount importance.

From the moment you enter the workforce, you will be challenged by such factors as the speed of change, technology, globalisation, market forces and competition to name a few. Those of you who respond positively and demonstrate a willingness to embrace all that comes will thrive, not merely survive.

Within the companies I have worked for, regardless in which part of the world they were based, I have seen the impact that change can have on the workplace, both from a positive and negative perspective. Product development, systems integration, restructures and the rise of the machines all influence the rate of change and provide challenges as well as amazing opportunities.

I have observed employees, managers and senior leaders respond both negatively and positively to change. Those that refuse to embrace change and don't have an open mind eventually leave the company, as a result of their own choices, or the company makes the decision for them.

If you refuse to acknowledge and embrace change, you will greatly limit your career potential. Ultimately, you set your own limits in terms of where you take your career and, for that matter, your life. Granted there are external factors that will have an influence on it which I affectionately call the three Cs.

Change + Choice + Chance = Career outcomes.
(Bruce Harkness 2018)

C + C + C = Career outcomes.

- **Change:** To transform or convert something from what it is or what it was. There are both internal and external influencers that have an impact on change, some of which you can control and some you cannot.
- **Choice:** Your right, opportunity or need to choose. Once again, there are both internal and external factors that influence the choices you make but you are accountable for these choices.
- **Chance:** Those wonderful moments in life where a chance meeting or opportunity presents itself. They are all around you and greatly influenced by your mindset and openness to receiving them.

The combination of these three Cs shapes the direction that both your career and your life will take. Regardless of the external influences such as change and chance, you ultimately decide how you perform at work. Yes, that's right: choice and the power to choose is an internal factor you can control in your career and ultimately your life. This is a very powerful realisation and something to keep in mind if you feel powerless to influence your life and career.

To build a successful and rewarding career is one of life's great opportunities and is made up of not one but many decisions over your career lifecycle. It is what you decide to do next that will make all the difference. So what will your next choice be? Regardless of what you decide on today, it is important to keep making decisions that will move you one step closer to your career vision.

However, when all is said and done, you are responsible for the choices you make and ultimately the mindset you choose to adopt. Maintaining sustained and high levels of performance in today's workplace is a challenge, as expectations are high and pressure to perform is even higher.

High performers in business focus on the development of a positive mindset as a priority. A positive or negative state of mind is ultimately derived from the choices you make each day. Whenever a high performer experiences a setback, they quickly move from a negative mindset to a positive solutions-focused mindset. This involves questioning themselves as to what they can learn from this situation in order to do better or to avoid a similar setback in the future. They display focus and resilience to bounce back to a positive mindset and move towards their goals once again.

People who enjoy sustained performance understand the virtue of a positive mindset. Most importantly, they understand innately that they are far more likely to achieve their goals with a positive point of view about the challenges they face.

Given that you will be working for at least half of your natural life, it is critical that you derive enjoyment from the work you do. It is also important to ensure that you maintain your performance levels (or edge as I like to call it) to ensure that you undertake your work to the best of your ability.

Reflection

1. Get to know yourself – the good the bad and the ugly – and continue to build your self-awareness throughout your life.

2. Identify what it is you are truly passionate about.

3. Develop a career and life plan and think about the legacy you want to leave.

4. Continue to learn and challenge yourself always.

5. Continually reinvent.

6. Surround yourself with positive people who want to see you succeed.

7. Develop confidence and self-belief.

8. Build your resilience.

9. Be grateful.

10. Look to the future; identify trends and opportunities and move towards them.

11. Persist and always learn from experience; failure is a natural part of the journey.

12. Strive to be the best possible version of your authentic self.

Chapter Two

Change, innovate or be gone

Increasingly, companies are becoming more and more dependent on technology and focusing on restructuring or right-sizing their workforce due to such influences as profit optimisation, competition, technological advancements and globalisation. Never before has the global economy been so volatile; a scenario which inevitably translates to the workplace. According to the World Economic Forum, by 2020 over five million jobs will be lost to robot technology alone. With a rapidly growing population and increasing periods of people's life spent working, I believe the most under-valued and overlooked pieces of the puzzle are those individuals who make up the cogs that turn the giant wheels of the global economy. Yes, that's right, those employees who turn strategy into reality and keep the mighty 'hamster wheel spinning'! In spite of technological advancements, the human factor will continue to remain a critical component of any business's success.

For any business to be able to survive turbulent times in a dynamic and unpredictable global market, the ability to adapt to change, and to focus on optimising all aspects of that business in terms of employee performance, has never been so important. This process starts with ensuring the right people are on board, and that they are aligned and engaged with the vision of the company they work for.

Your contribution goes way beyond the profits of the company you work for. The spill-over benefit from what you do in the form of the taxes you pay, and the services and products your company produces make a contribution way beyond your actual job. Yet, your job is an essential part of the puzzle for as long as you, and the job itself, continue to add value. To be employed is in itself a contribution to the economy and society in which you live. Therefore, it is true to say that with employment comes a responsibility beyond merely clocking in and clocking out of your workplace each day.

The success of any company is a direct result of the people who work in it, regardless of what they produce or what service they provide. The ever-changing landscape of business which has been fast tracked in the aftermath of the Global Financial Crisis and the prevailing uncertainty of a fragile global economy has placed unprecedented financial, operational and technological challenges on businesses and those people who work in them.

Subsequently, the pressure to perform at all levels within businesses, from customer-facing employees to senior business leaders has never been so great. Now more than ever we are working harder and longer, with longer hours largely driven by the expectation to be accessible via the ever-present personal device. These expectations from business owners and shareholders can be summarised simply as 'more for less': more profits and leaner company structures.

This new reality is derived from lessons learnt during the Global Financial Crisis in which many companies' employee numbers exceeded their actual needs. This learning, combined with the current economic climate which can at best be described as fragile, has forced companies into a 'more for less' mindset. What is concerning is that many organisations have failed to prepare their workforce for this new dynamic and simply continue to 'squeeze the lemon' as opposed to giving a clear rationale as to the reasons why and, more importantly, to involving their workforce in the solution.

Given the uncertain and fragile economic climate (which is likely to continue to be both fragile and volatile), this uncertainty combined with the daily pressures placed on employees in the workplace, creates a pressure cooker that is called Life. How do you ensure, or at least increase, your chances of career survival and success in such a precarious environment?

The reality is that the majority of us are totally unprepared to navigate through this 'perfect storm'.

Even those of us fortunate to have jumped through the hoops of 12 to 18 years of education and run the gauntlet of early career turbulence are no wiser or closer to truly understanding how to manage our careers or how best to optimise our chances of success and ultimately perform to our full potential. The gradual rise in recent years understanding the value of business coaching within the workplace, as well as of leadership development, has provided valuable support for those individuals lucky enough to have access to this type of professional and personal growth. In addition, it has better equipped them to manage their careers and perform at a higher level.

However, the harsh reality is that the vast majority of employees within organisations do not have access to this type of professional career development. In fact, it is often reserved for those individuals within the organisation who already occupy senior leadership roles and who are deemed to be talented enough to have the potential to go on and assume greater levels of responsibility. On the whole, business coaching seems to be reserved for a limited few within the workplace, despite its multiple benefits, including the opportunity to increase self-awareness, develop leadership capability, establish goals and job priorities, as well as exploration of workplace relationships which can be extremely challenging for an individual.

More often than not, the narrow application of business coaching has limited impact on most organisations in terms of building a high-performance culture because it targets a very select few individuals and does not always take a strength-based approach. I strongly believe that to create a true performance-driven and winning culture, CEOs and senior leadership need to engage every level of the business to focus on building their personal brand and workplace performance.

Sustainable organisational change and the opportunity to build a true performance-focused culture is a leadership responsibility that is won and lost 'on the shop floor'.

Regardless of the size of the company you work for, the mantra is as simple as it is complex: 'more for less'. Yes, that's right – more for less. You are and will continue to be expected to work harder, often with fewer resources and less people to get the job done. Less does not figure in any company's strategic or financial plan. 'Why?' I hear you cry. Because rightly or wrongly capitalism, the global economy, investors' and shareholders' expectations are based on more. Customers want more, you want more; more drives business or it will until such time as we reach a tipping point where more loses its appeal or becomes unattainable. In the meantime, what you can expect is for everyone to expect more; less does not figure anywhere in the equation.

Leadership needs to engage all levels of a company in the vision and direction they are taking their staff, as they set the performance bar high. In addition, they should be role models for the performance and behaviours they would like to see occur within the business. Those organisations that are successful focus on the development of leadership qualities and capability, and empower the workforce at every level within the business. Most importantly, they recruit people who are passionate about what it is the business does and who have an exceptional attitude. An excellent example of this is the company Patagonia which CEO Yvon Chouinard developed as a result of his passion for climbing and the outdoors. From a cultural perspective, Patagonia has always endeavoured to recruit people who are passionate about the outdoors and the strong ethos and authentic culture that Yvon Chouinard founded the company on.

I would like to take this opportunity to reflect upon the topic of leadership. Why? Because in the workplace, leadership matters; it has a strong influence on everything in a business. To be honest, I have lost count of the number of articles and books I have read on the subject of leadership and the number of lists highlighting the qualities that leaders should display. Ultimately, my view is that the subject of leadership has become 'over baked'.

Excellence in leadership starts and finishes with an innate desire to put the needs of others before your own and to move those whom you inspire to follow you towards a vision that represents a better place.

In my opinion, humility, empathy and gratitude are the most important qualities of true leaders. However, many companies lack future-orientated leadership, so the greatest challenge for companies today is the recruitment, development and retention of high-quality leaders.

The pursuit of leadership for self-interest is flawed and rarely results in sustained performance. Leadership is a privilege and excellence in leadership starts with the effective management of one's self. I sincerely believe that you are a leader if you choose to be one. Adopting a leadership mindset is also a choice and some of the most inspiring leadership I have observed originates from the most unlikely places within companies. You do not need permission to lead and to behave as a leader.

Consider this for a moment: I estimate that for professional sports people, coaching and continuous development in their chosen sport represents more than two thirds of their sporting career in terms of a commitment in time. On average, at the highest levels, a sportsperson's career lasts for seven years. You may find this next statistic overwhelming: in the Western World the average working lifespan is 45 years. Yes that's right – 45 years! However, it is rare for most individuals to have access to coaching and structured professional development during their working lives. Yet, they will be expected to perform to the best of their ability, day in and day out.

With that in mind, it is in your best interests to ensure that you continue to grow both professionally and personally over the course of your working life, raising the bar just a little higher each year. Let's face it, given the amount of time you will spend in the workplace you may as well give it your very best efforts. In fact, if you don't you are wasting some of the most precious years of your life.

In this new age of uncertainty, the importance of improving your performance, understanding and leveraging your strengths, as well as creating a powerful and authentic personal brand has never been so important!

For those of you currently enjoying a level of career success, complacency is your greatest threat! Once you win the title fight the most difficult part is to retain the championship belt. So how will you maintain your edge to ensure you continue to perform? And, more importantly, what goals have you set for the future to take you to the next level?

Reflection

1. Self-development is a personal choice but ignore it at your peril.

2. Beware of complacency and avoid it at all costs.

3. You do not need permission to be a leader.

4. Tomorrow's leaders will be highly self-aware and display empathy, humility and gratitude.

5. Continually develop your leadership capability.

6. Understand that change is constant and the mantra of 'more for less' is here to stay.

Chapter Three

Riding the change train

The choices you made in your past need not be a predictor of the outcomes in your future.

The harsh reality is that career survival is a precarious journey and a long one – provided all goes well. In the age of the 'knowledge worker' and as the world's economy continues to move on at lightning speed from the last remnants of the Industrial Age, we are all riding the 'change bullet train' and striving to survive in a highly volatile and competitive environment. The risk of company restructures and subsequent redundancies are a daily reality in the workplace. Quite simply, many of you will find, or are currently finding it overwhelming to keep up with the speed that organisations require to move forward to ensure their own survival.

The topic of change has been well-researched and what emerges as a common theme is that change itself is inevitable. Consequently, it is important not to fight it; rather, learn to embrace it and enjoy the opportunities that change can bring, particularly if you are open to it! What is perhaps more apparent is that the speed of change the world is currently experiencing is unprecedented from an economic, political and environmental perspective. Business cycles are shorter and the workplace has become more unpredictable; there is less job security and more demands in terms of performance, the impact of emerging technology and the constant refinement of work practices.

Some futurists have indicated it is likely that the next 10 to 15 years will witness more change than the past one thousand years, with technology, globalisation, climate change and an increasingly competitive world market being some of the biggest influencers. And that's not even taking into account such factors as terrorism and political upheaval. As a result of this chaos, a spill-over effect into the workplace is inevitable.

I admire Faith Popcorn and the work she does as CEO of the Brain Reserve. Faith predicts that beyond the influence of technology, the impact of robotics on humanity will be substantial and the subsequent impact on the workplace will be equally significant. I believe the compounding challenge from a career and business perspective is that organisations and those individuals working within them are not prepared at present for the rate and complexity of the change that is currently at play.

So, with these dynamics in mind, how can you not only survive but also increase your chances of achieving career success in the workplace? Within the following pages, you will have an opportunity to reflect upon and explore a range of questions that will greatly enhance your chances of achieving your own definition of success, as well as developing your personal brand. In addition, you will be in a better position to optimise your impact, influence and performance in the workplace.

Some of you may be asking the question: Why is this important? Consider this: given that the average human life span is approximately 76 years with 45 of these being dedicated to work, my question is: Why wouldn't you give it your best shot? I struggle with the idea of giving anything less than 100% of my best effort every day. Obviously, some days are better than others and you will experience both highs and lows in both your work and life. This is ok; as long as effort and good intent are present that is what really matters.

As previously mentioned, we are deeply immersed in the new and exciting age of the 'knowledge worker' – an age in which change, technology and globalisation reign supreme. Customer expectations are higher than ever before and profit margins have never been so tight. The way in which we work and the way businesses operate today was thought to be impossible less than a decade ago. From a business perspective, it is 'mission critical' for companies to embrace change and to grow and develop. Outsourcing, offshoring, virtual meetings across multiple time zones and shared economies are now firmly embedded in today's workplace. Those of you who work within large or small companies must adapt to this changing environment or run the risk of getting left behind … or worse still becoming extinct.

Technology is an immensely strong driver of change in business and greatly influences the speed at which business is done. It also significantly affects how and when you communicate with your colleagues, customers and suppliers. The importance of understanding how to use technology effectively and leveraging it to your advantage within the workplace is a critical survival skill.

The various devices and supporting Apps you have at your disposal are intended to keep you connected and increase both your connectivity and productivity in the workplace. Nevertheless, overreliance and misuse of these tools is not effective use of technology. Don't be fooled – working in an environment where you are sending emails while browsing the internet and responding to your last SMS is not effective use of technology or your time. In fact, that type of workplace behaviour will inevitably make you less effective and productive, despite providing you with short bursts of instant gratification.

In Cal Newport's book *Deep Work* he discusses a Harvard study involving a group of management consultants who were adamant that constant connection to their email was necessary for them to effectively service their clients. When forced to disconnect more regularly as part of the research study, they discovered that constant access to emails did not matter nearly as much as they had assumed. You will find that your colleagues will also welcome less emails and more face-to-face discussion. So, once again, embrace technology; don't fight it but be careful not to abuse, overuse or become over reliant on it. Be curious, keep yourself up-to-date with current work practices and where possible take time to learn about emerging technology and trends.

The value of having a strong and authentic personal brand both within the company where you currently work and outside this organisation has never been so important.

By definition, when I say 'personal brand', I mean the skills, capability, value and reputation you have within your industry.

Your personal brand influences the perceptions your colleagues have of you. Most importantly, how you communicate and interact with others has a big impact on your reputation and the perceptions others have of you. At this point, I would also like to stress the importance of consistent behaviour. Inconsistent behaviour creates confusion, suspicion and a loss of credibility in most cases.

Today's workplace is intensely competitive and globalisation and technological innovation have greatly increased the number of people applying for available jobs. In fact, competition for your job can now come from practically anywhere in the world and, increasingly, you are competing with emerging technology which may threaten or replace your job in the future. Regardless of how you feel about this change, the speed of change and the compounding effect of globalisation will continue to evolve and intensify over time as emerging economies 'look for their place in the sun'.

The first step in building your resilience to cope with the competitive nature of the workplace and cultivating a successful career is to accept that change is here to stay, that change is good and that, ultimately, you can become a 'change maker'!

It is important to take time not only to understand the nature of the changes that are occurring but also to constantly seek opportunities to jump onto the 'change bullet train' and up-skill yourself. By following this approach, you will ensure you develop the relevant skillset and knowledge to take advantage of the change that is upon you.

Those of you who learn to anticipate and respond well to change will be best positioned to react and seek new and exciting opportunities. Initially, this can be difficult as change can be confronting and can create feelings of uncertainty. Hanging on to what has passed often leads to frustration and anxiety. By letting go and embracing the moment you will feel better prepared and will create the opportunity to be open to whatever new things change may bring.

Our ability to let go readily is influenced by what psychologists call locus of control. This concept, developed by Julian B. Rotter in 1954, essentially suggests that people who have a dominant internal locus of control believe the outcomes of their life are influenced by the decisions that they make compared with those individuals with a dominant external locus of control who believe it is predominately external influences that shape their lives.

Buddha said, 'The mind is everything. What you think, you become'. Regardless of what you believe in terms of your ability to control your life, the one thing you have no control over is change. Ultimately, the daily choices you make provide you with the greatest potential to influence the direction your future life will take. Thankfully, the choices you made in your past need not be a predictor for outcomes in your future. Each new moment provides a unique and precious opportunity to make decisions that can take your career and life in a new and exciting direction.

The Millennials will work harder and longer than previous generations and the separation between work, family and leisure will become less. In my opinion, the concept of a work life balance is obsolete and the new frontier is finding your own personal balance. What works for you may be very different to the next person.

By now I think you will agree that change is constant and the pressure to perform in the workplace is intense as the business environment becomes increasingly more competitive. Career success and ultimately workplace survival requires you to think and act way beyond the boundaries of your job description. With this in mind, I would like to pose the hypothesis: *If you can think and act like an entrepreneur within the company you work for, you will fundamentally change the way you view the business and how you approach your job.*

Giving yourself permission to think and act like an entrepreneur can greatly increase your engagement and the satisfaction you derive from your work. Quite simply, there is no room for mediocrity in business today. If you want to succeed and ultimately realise your full potential, you need to commit to your role as if the company was your own start-up business.

Success has always belonged to those people who are prepared to go beyond what is expected.

It goes further than simply being dedicated and passionate; you must be relentless in the pursuit of your vision of success.

The pressure to perform at work has a corresponding impact on the work environment, more often than not emerging as high employee turnover, increased absenteeism and stress-related claims against companies.

Without doubt, the physical and mental impact of stress is significant and well-documented. The effects of workplace stress include anxiety, depression, fatigue, burnout, negative impacts on social behaviour, cardiovascular disease and metabolic syndrome. The list goes on. Working longer or at least being connected to the workplace beyond normal working hours is now a reality and presenteeism is becoming the new cultural norm in many companies. My definition of presenteeism is being present at your workplace beyond reasonable working hours but not necessarily being productive. Stressed employees who are fearful about losing their jobs are often more present from a time perspective but far less engaged and productive. As a side point, and from my own experience in business, it is those employees who fail to embrace change, truly engage with their company and build their skill capability to be successful within the work place who most often become stressed.

Almost every human resources journal I have read or conference I have attended make reference to the cost of a poorly performing workforce. I recall hearing at one particular conference that the cost of an individual employee performing poorly sits somewhere between 6 to 15 times the value of their annualised salary. That said, I have no doubt that the actual impact of an under-performing employee is very difficult to actually calculate. What is certain, however, is that under performance and lack of engagement of any workforce has a detrimental impact on the culture of that organisation, its financial performance, the quality of the products it produces or the service it provides. The end result is that both the customer and the company suffer significantly. If you fall into the category of an underperformer, the spill-over effect on your personal brand is that your internal and external market value and your appeal to future employers are greatly devalued.

Reflection

1. The only certainty in the age of the 'knowledge worker' is change.

2. It is important not only to embrace change but to anticipate it and identify the opportunities it brings.

3. Within the workplace, expectations to perform are high and both companies and employees alike must 'perform or be gone'.

4. By understanding the value of your personal brand and viewing what you do within your organisation through the eyes of an entre-preneur, your satisfaction levels, motivation, engagement and performance in the work-place will improve.

Chapter Four

Embracing chaos

The chaos which surrounds us is not a one-off event. It is ever present and provides endless possibilities.

As engineer and economist Klaus Schwab once said, 'We are moving from a world in which the big eat the small to a world in which the fast eat the slow'. Those people who will not only survive but thrive will be the ones who commit their hearts and minds to the job that needs to be done. Your commitment to your job, team and company must be nothing short of 100%. Both your team and the leadership of the company you work for can very easily sense if you are not committed. Excellence cannot be faked!

Commit to being exceptional at what you do. If you don't, those people who are willing to do so will walk right over the top of you.

Another compelling reason for committing to excellence is that you will avoid damaging your personal brand. This, in turn, will prevent a negative impact on your work, team and, ultimately, the culture and performance of the company itself. Don't waste your own time or your employers'. Step aside and allow someone else to have a go. Change, innovate or be gone.

To survive and excel in today's marketplace, companies must be highly adaptable, lean in structure and fast in terms of decision-making processes. Technology and the application of supporting processes is 'mission critical'. However, above all, the need to be adaptable is crucial. Bureaucracy and hierarchy have no place in high-performing companies. Leaders need to be highly adaptable and have the ability to embrace change, as well as being innovative, visionary, people-focused, resilient and authentic in terms of how they lead their business toward a shared vision. Slow and steady will not make the grade!

Those organisations that adapt will survive and those that don't will quite simply become extinct. Regardless of technological development, it is people who drive change within companies and the effectiveness of how that change is managed is dependent on the quality of leadership and talent that exists within those very organisations. As we boldly move into an uncertain and increasingly competitive future, the way we work must change. Needless and lengthy reporting, senseless repetitive administration and protracted approval processes have no place in today's hyper-fast economy. These processes do nothing to satisfy customer expectations regardless of the industry!

To ensure that you catch the 'change bullet train' you must be prepared to commit to your job and the company you work for while at the same time ensuring that you develop yourself both professionally and personally through relevant training and experience-based learning. Good companies will provide formal and informal training in addition to learning opportunities. However, don't expect anyone else to take charge of your personal development – ultimately that's your responsibility. So take charge of your self-development and, above all, avoid having a mindset that is resistant to learning or being influenced by any individuals within your organisation or network who are resistant to change. They will hold you back from realising your true potential and will gradually wear you down to their way of thinking. Remember, the Dodo bird became extinct because it failed to adapt to its changing environment!

Ok, now let's press the pause button for a moment and think back to the time when you started your first job. Do you remember how you felt when you initially secured that new and exciting opportunity? It was most likely a sense of heightened excitement and feeling that: 'I am going to change the world!' Well, it's that winning feeling that you need to embrace, protect and nurture every single day!

We live in an age where enough is never enough and the fundamentals of capitalism feed this paradigm relentlessly.

Marketers and advertising agencies leverage this principle and business budgets are built on the promise of growth. Some people may suggest it is what distinguishes us as a species: the relentless pursuit to go beyond where we currently are. But regardless of your opinion on this topic, those individuals who will continue to thrive, as opposed to merely survive, will be those who understand these dynamics. Those individuals who resist this reality will be swept aside by organisations that are looking for future talent to lead their companies and who understand the reality of the world in which we live and the changes the future will bring.

Traditional career paths no longer exist and 25-year careers in the same company are quite simply a remnant of the Industrial Age. In the 'knowledge worker' age, employees will move between full-time roles, consulting gigs, contract and part-time work, interspersed with periods of unemployment. Like it or not, this is the landscape we inhabit and it will remain so for the foreseeable future. In order to future-proof your career plan, you will need to start to develop awareness and acceptance of this reality and foster a positive mindset to deal with uncertainty and change. This will become a critical skill to develop to ensure your future success.

Empower yourself and take charge of your own career and personal development. Great companies, of course, will continue to invest in top talent, track their progress and plan for their future growth and professional development. However, most companies simply don't have the necessary time or resources to manage talent development and career planning.

Navigating the 'ups and downs' of your career involves focusing on what you can control and not what you cannot. Keep this principle firmly in your mind. You need to develop a mindset which involves taking charge of your own destiny while accepting the fact that it is always subject to change. In the following chapters we will explore a range of ideas which are designed to greatly help you with this process. However, in these early stages, what is most important is for you to increase your self-awareness in terms of your openness to accepting change, committing to it, as well as taking ownership of your career.

Companies need their employees at every level to think, speak and behave like entrepreneurs. Why is this so?

Today's companies are flatter and leaner in terms of their structure and hierarchy, and profit targets are set increasingly higher. The only way for any company to truly realise its full potential in this environment is to ensure that the entire organisation is pulling in the same direction. This is no longer optional – just in case you might have been thinking otherwise! What this means is that you need to avoid merely coming to work but, rather, fundamentally, to take ownership of your role and philosophically align your thinking and work practices with those of the company you work for. In this way, you should consider that you are the company.

For some of you this will be a significant shift in your mindset. The 'why' for this change in perception is as follows: if you are not able to adopt this mindset with your existing company, you should start to consider changing your mindset or moving to another company that you truly identify with. If you don't, you run the risk of becoming disengaged and, ultimately, underperforming in your job, which is bad for the company and bad for your personal brand reputation.

Those individuals who will enjoy long-term career satisfaction and success will not only have the above mentioned mindset but also be highly adaptable, solutions-focused, entrepreneurial and self-motivated. The benefits of adopting the mindset of an entrepreneur when you engage with your company are considerable. Not only will it help you to understand how your role fits within the organisation you work for, you will also start to understand the big picture through the eyes of your company as if it were your own. In addition, you will be able to identify opportunities that will benefit the company and add real value to your personal brand reputation, your team and the company you work for. Finally, you will start to understand what it actually takes to drive a business and move it towards greatness which, in turn, can greatly increase your market value. In simple terms, this is how much a company is willing to pay you.

In this way, it is apparent that the rules of work have changed and are constantly changing at a rate that is hard to comprehend. So what does this mean for you? How do you mange that dynamic? How can you thrive in this environment? What steps can you take today that will make a difference for you now and for your long-term future? It is important to have an open mind when addressing the above questions. In her book *Mindset,* world-renown Stanford University psychologist Carol Dweck explores the idea of growth mindset versus fixed mindset. More specifically, Dweck's research identifies that those people with a growth mindset have a greater tendency to outperform those with a fixed mindset.

In essence, someone with a growth mindset is open to change, new learning and the belief that they can continue to develop and grow as an individual. A fixed mindset is in opposition to this and these individuals are resistant to growth and new learning. In addition, those people who have a fixed mindset tend to be more self-doubting. Dweck's work is particularly interesting because it highlights that a certain mindset can fundamentally change the course of an individual's career and life. Dweck found that the development of either a fixed or growth mindset starts during our infancy. Encouragingly, Dweck also found that it is possible to shift our mindset even as adults.

According to Dweck, 'My research has shown that the view you adopt for yourself profoundly affects the way you lead your life'. Regardless of the environment in which you live, the upbringing you had, the education you received, the relationships you have been in and the role models you may or may not have had in your life, how you choose to think rests largely with you. Your conscious choice is the greatest determinant of whether you have a fixed or growth mindset or an optimistic or pessimistic outlook on life.

I have always believed that your past need not be a predictor of your future. Self-belief, optimism and a growth mindset are all behaviours that you can consciously choose to adopt. In the workplace and life, if you don't belief in yourself, you can almost guarantee that the people you interact with will not believe in you either.

Psychologist Angela Lee Duckworth's research into 'grit' which she defines as 'passion and perseverance towards long-term goals' has a tendency to have a direct link with those people who are more likely to succeed as opposed to those who are not. Furthermore, she found that an above average IQ, physical health, good looks and social intelligence are in no way a guarantee of success. It is grit that is the key behaviour which determines sustained success and, in combination with a growth mindset, significantly and positively influences the long-term achievement of goals.

Working in the field of positive psychology, Shawn Achor has identified that happiness – the way in which you perceive the world, your life and the challenges you face – has a direct impact on your chances of success. Once again, happiness is largely a product of mindset and can be developed through repetitive and continuous practice. Achor proposes that people who are happy are 23% less stressed, on average enjoy 39% better health, are 31% more productive and enjoy 34% more positive social interactions.

Achor believes that it is possible to foster happiness through systematic practice which includes writing down three things each day you are grateful for; writing a daily journal entry about a positive experience, participating in 15 minutes of daily mindful cardio activity, meditating daily and engaging in one daily act of random kindness. Achor suggests that if you apply this process for 21 days you will begin to see a lasting shift in your mindset towards being more positive.

What is common to the research conducted by Dweck, Duckworth and Achor is that we can change our mindset through both conscious choice and repetitive action. By doing so, you will greatly enhance your chances of enjoying a happy and successful career and life.

Reflection

1. Your past need not be a predictor of your future.

2. Believing in yourself and adopting a growth mindset is ultimately a personal choice and will greatly increase your chances of sustained success.

3. Applying 'grit' which can be interpreted as 'unrelenting determination towards achieving your goals' is a powerful behaviour that will significantly increase your likelihood of achieving success.

4. Happiness can be practiced and has a significant positive impact on your overall wellbeing and chances of success.

Chapter Five

Blow up the box

In today's world, merely thinking outside the box is not enough. Blow the damn thing up and start again.

If there is one phrase that makes me squirm it's: 'We need to think outside the box'. Agh! 'Blow it up and start again!' I say. The reality is that most of us spend the majority of our waking hours at work. In addition to our work, we also manage a multitude of other commitments, including family, relationships, financial commitments ... and let's face it life itself.

As we have previously explored, companies are moving and changing at (almost) the speed of light. What is of critical importance is that we take time out not only to evaluate our performance but also to put together an action plan that will dramatically improve our performance and satisfaction levels at work.

In the following chapters, through a process of self-reflection, you will have the opportunity to:

- Improve your performance in your current job regardless of what it may be.
- Consider in-depth your own personal definition of success and commit to it.
- Identify your strengths and map out your career path.
- Understand and build your personal brand value.

The way in which success is defined will be very different from one person to the next. A sports car in the driveway, financial freedom, that dream holiday, giving to others, having a family … the list goes on. To assist you in defining your definition of success I would like to share my own definition with you.

Success involves choosing exactly what it is that you want to achieve and then being able to achieve it!

Sounds simple, right? Why then is it so difficult to identify what success looks like from both a career and life perspective? How many people in your workplace do you know have a clear picture of what success looks like? Success does not magically appear as a result of good luck. Success must be pursued systematically and relentlessly through the alignment of passion, focus, resilience, determination and sheer hard work.

In his book *8 to be Great: the 8 traits that successful people have in common,* Richard St. John describes how he dedicated 10 years of his life to researching what it takes to be successful. Over a 10 year period, St. John conducted 500 face-to-face interviews with a wide range of successful people, including Bill Gates, Richard Branson, Chris Rock, Muhammad Ali, Tom Hanks, Warren Buffet, Jennifer Lopez, Oprah Winfrey and Martha Stewart. In addition, he studied thousands of other success stories.

The eight character traits that Richard St. John identified successful people displayed are:

1. Passion
2. Hard working
3. Focused
4. Ability to push themselves

5. Ability to generate ideas
6. Willingness to improve
7. Service to others
8. Motivation to persist.

While St. John's research is compelling, at this point in your career, regardless of whether your position is the CEO or an undergraduate, the first step you need to take is to create your own compelling definition of success. This is the starting point and will ultimately provide you with direction. Although you may have previously done this, when was the last time you truly reflected upon it?

The purpose of this exercise is to prompt you to deliberate beyond where you currently are. You may ask, 'Why is this important?' Regardless of your age demographic and your philosophy on life, successful people have a vision and a journey map to help them achieve what they want from their working lives. And your career is no different. If you apply St John's 8 traits of successful people, you will have an opportunity to further increase your chances of achieving success.

Take a moment now to ask yourself and to reflect upon the question: What is your definition of success? Once you have crafted your definition of success it will be a lot easier for you to set objectives that will move you towards it. Be sure to set the bar high as this is a great opportunity to move you closer to reaching your full potential.

Your definition of success

Depending on where you obtain your data, the average working life can be somewhere between 45 to 50 years ... and for some people it may be even longer! If you are passionate about what you do, then work is merely an extension of a rich and wonderful life so you may well be happy to continue working for as long as possible.

In his book *Re-imagine! Business excellence in a disruptive age* Tom Peters writes about 'Brand You'.

According to Peters, 'If there is nothing very special about your work, no matter how hard you apply yourself you won't get noticed, and that increasingly means you won't get paid much either'. He also states that 'You are the story teller of your own life, and you can create your own legend or not'.

In addressing this first important question, you will need to move from reflex (i.e. I want to earn lots of money) to reflection (i.e. what legacy do I want to leave and what do I want to achieve in my career?). From my own perspective, I have been fortunate in both my personal life and career to have met some amazing and successful people. Those people I have met who have achieved their definition of success or were well on their way to achieving it, enjoy a level of material wealth but, most importantly, they are rich beyond their wildest dreams in terms of living a life that is more meaningful. In addition, they are making a contribution beyond their own needs while enjoying more happiness in their working life and are exceedingly grateful for it! True success in work and life need not be limited to wealth; it's much bigger than that in my opinion. Making a contribution and moving towards achieving your full potential are priceless.

Now let's take a moment to think about your career and, more specifically, your career vision. This is your opportunity to not only think big but also align your definition of success with the vision you have for your career. Give yourself permission to dream and don't place limits on what your career vision could be.

At this point in time, I encourage you to put this book down. Yes, that's right – put it down! Go for a walk; enjoy being in a natural environment that inspires you and reflect deeply upon your definition of career success. There is real value in taking time out of your daily environment to be in Nature – free from technology and the hustle of daily life. You should take time out to be in silence in order to truly reflect.

In the documentary, *The Pursuit of Silence* the benefits of silence and nature on health, wellbeing and happiness are explored. Some of the benefits mentioned include a reduction in anxiety levels, improved immunity and memory, increased feelings of overall wellbeing and happiness, as well as improved concentration. Further research from the Nippon Medical School in Tokyo shows that a walk in nature changes blood flow to the brain and promotes a state of relaxation.

The benefits are real and extremely beneficial. So take a moment to invest in yourself and further challenge yourself to commit to making this immersion in nature a daily (or at least weekly) event. To reap the rewards it can be as simple as taking a walk in your local park. Take your time; there is no need to rush this step in the process. Note down a couple of definitions and options. Discuss your thoughts with a trusted friend, partner or mentor. Challenge yourself to set the bar high – in fact, remove the damn bar! Once you have thoughtfully crafted your personal career vision, I encourage you to pick up this book once again and continue on your career transformation journey.

Your career vision

_____

_____

_____

_____

_____

_____

_____

Welcome back! Now that you have meticulously crafted your definition of career success, another important question to ponder upon is 'Why?'. Why is it important to go through this process? Asking the question 'Why?' will allow you to understand exactly where you are in terms of your career evolution right now. Do you want to fast track your career or leverage your current role in order to secure your next opportunity? Or are you stagnating in your current role and looking to move on?

In order to navigate effectively to your next destination it is critical that you understand where you currently are in your career. In other words, asking the question 'Why?' will provide you with the answer and motivation to move from where you currently are to where you would ultimately like to be.

Why do I want to commit to this vision?

_____

_____

_____

_____

_____

The question 'Why?' is extremely important because it will give you a sense of purpose and reason to move onto the next step of your career journey. Yes that's right. You need to move and that could be both at a physical and psychological level. A change in your physical location and mindset can help you on your way to the next stage in your career and, indeed, your life. Change is good!

We are living in what is often referred to as a VUCA world – a world in which there are high levels of volatility, uncertainty, complexity and ambiguity. Now more than ever before it is important to *avoid stagnation in your career at all cost as stagnation and complacency are the ultimate evil for the knowledge worker.*

Achieving any level of success requires sustained drive and momentum. Developing the ability to be solutions-focused, to keep learning and evolving, being prepared to change and having the courage to explore new opportunities and maintain an open mind to deal with significant challenges are all critical skills to cultivate.

The significant problems we have cannot be solved at the same level of thinking at which we created them.
– Albert Einstein

Why you do what you do is an extremely important question to ask yourself in order to find deeper meaning in your career. The question of 'Why?' is equally important for companies to ponder. Simon Sinek has pioneered the idea of 'Start With Why'. He explores the power of organisations asking themselves the question: Why do we do what we do? Most organisations know what and how they do what they do, but very few really understand why they do what they do. And the same can be said for the vast majority of employees who work within these companies.

Insightful leadership recognises the importance of investing cold, hard currency into understanding and creating a vision around the question of 'Why?'. By defining the 'Why?' for your career, you will have a compelling reason to engage in your own personal career vision.

Generally speaking, in most companies the process of creating the organisation's vision is a top-down approach from a hierarchy perspective. However, some companies take time to survey and engage their employees to help create a vision and actively play a part in answering the question of 'Why?'. This results in far higher levels of engagement from the workforce and, indeed, better product, service and profit outcomes.

If you can find a link between your personal 'Why do you do what you do?' and the why of the company you work for, you are also more likely to authentically engage with your workplace. Unfortunately, employee engagement in most companies is actually quite low. A Forbes Magazine article written by Joseph Folkman refers to a 2013 research study on employee engagement undertaken by the Gallup organisation in which it was noted that 7 out of 10 workers in America are either actively disengaged or not engaged in their work. Regardless of your opinion regarding this statistic, it is certainly an alarming number! With this in mind, I believe it makes perfect sense that, from a personal and career perspective, the question 'Why?' is something you should explore in some detail at various points during your career in order to see if it still holds true with the company that you are currently working for or aspire to work for in the future.

For many people, obsessing over what they do as opposed to understanding and finding meaning in 'why they do what they do' seems to be the norm. At a societal level, the question 'What do you do?' is yet another form of validation in terms of how you define yourself and how others perceive you. The perennial question of 'So what do you do for a living?' is often the go-to question at social gatherings and a way in which, as a society, we pigeon-hole others. However, by finding meaning in 'Why you do what you do' as opposed to defining yourself by 'What you do' is often far more powerful at a personal level. So why not drop the ego and at your next social gathering ask a far more interesting question: Why do you do what you do?

Don't get me wrong. The question 'What?' still has a place and is a logical next question to reflect upon. What is the primary goal that you're hoping to achieve as a result of going through this process? Think carefully as it might just open the door to a wonderful new and exciting opportunity for you. Examples could be as diverse as securing your next career opportunity or taking the mighty leap of faith to open your own business. Regardless of the answer, the goal or goals that you set yourself should be succinct and measurable in terms of both time and actions in order to effectively move you one step closer to your vision of success.

What is your primary career goal or goals?

As with any well-crafted goal, it is important to set some specific actions and realistic timeframes as part of the process. Whether it is three months, six months or twelve months (but not more), you need to be able to see the goal clearly and track your progress as you move towards it. Your timeframe should be realistic and the actions both achievable and measurable, even if it's a case of simply identifying if it's done or not done. Above all, you must hold yourself accountable every step of the way. This is important and should not be underestimated as it is too easy to let deadlines pass by and rationalise as to why you did not complete a specific task or action. To put it simply, you must commit to getting it done!

Setting short and mid-term goals supported by relevant actions will greatly increase your chances of achieving success. Nevertheless, planning any more than twelve months ahead to achieve your next goal is too far away to really drive performance or to sustain your motivation to keep striving towards your goals. Keep your goals in 'mind's reach'. You must be able to see an end date that is not too far into the future or the goal becomes purely aspirational.

A research study was undertaken by Dr Gail Matthews, which included 267 participants from a variety of businesses and networking groups throughout the United States and overseas to find out how goal achievement in the workplace was influenced by physically writing down goals and committing to goal-directed actions and then taking personal accountability for those actions. In this study, it was found that more than 70% of the participants who sent weekly updates to a friend reported successful goal achievement. That is, they either completely accomplished their goal or were more than halfway there compared with 35% who did not write their goals down or share them with others. Physically writing your goals down and sharing them with others significantly increases your chances of achieving them.

Business and life move quickly and with job tenures continuing to decrease you can expect to change your job every 3.4 years according to statistics released by The Household, Income and Labour Dynamics in Australia. Over the course of someone's career lifespan this means that you may have up to 17 different jobs. Another increasing trend is the emergence of part-time employment and short-term contract work. Workplace agreements are becoming more dynamic and fluid which means that you need to be nimble in terms of managing your career. The road ahead is long and full of change, chance and opportunity, so keep your eyes on the horizon but remember to be mindful of the steps you take along the way.

At this stage, you should take time to reflect on your first steps, which are to understand where you currently are and to decide what direction you want to go, as opposed to trying to achieve your career vision in one mighty leap. If you have reflected deeply and created a vision that is truly inspirational, it will take time and a lot of hard work to get there. While time is a limited resource, you should consider that your career and working life are an ultra–marathon rather than a sprint.

My passion is leadership and talent development. When working with and observing high-performing leaders over the years, I have seen that those individuals who take the time to diligently craft and define a clear and compelling vision of success, supported by short and mid-term goals, as well as concise and relevant actions and timeframes, consistently achieve great outcomes. However, the real game-changer is that they have the ability make a conscious decision to commit to their vision and accept failure as merely another step on their journey to success. They accept responsibility, learn from their mistakes, record their goals and reflections, and review their progress on a regular basis.

Reflection

1. Outlining your definition of success and setting tangible goals shouldn't be a solitary process.

2. Seeking wise counsel from those whom you trust or establishing a mentoring relationship will enhance your thought processes and challenge you to think beyond your normal comfort zone.

3. Success of any description is rarely achieved while being in a comfortable physical or mental state. Often the most significant personal growth and learning is the result of facing or dealing with a challenge that takes an individual way beyond their normal comfort levels.

4. Achieving the goals you set is ultimately your responsibility.

5. Look to those people you deem to be successful; respect and value their opinion. Listen to them, talk to them, work with them and, most importantly, learn from them.

6. Build your support team, they are an important aspect of your journey; this could include your current manager, a team member or a trusted friend or family member. If you have not yet identified at least one person, get busy and seek them out at all cost!

Chapter Six

Know thyself

There are decisions that can change your life for the better. All you have to do is identify what they are and then make them.

At this stage, it's important to take some time to explore the advantages of developing greater levels of self-awareness. In other words, it is crucial for you to understand who you are and how you have arrived at your current career destination.

How do you become successful? This is a question I have been asked many times by a range of people in different countries all over the world. As a result of my work and travels, I have had the pleasure of meeting some of the most inspirational and gifted individuals anyone could hope to meet. I am not talking about PhD and MBA graduates or senior executives in business. I am talking about individuals who don't necessarily have higher level education but are special in terms of how they think about and view the world. They dare to challenge normal patterns of thinking and possess that rare alignment between their talents and their passions.

That said, I have also met some highly successful and passionate people with PhDs and MBAs from some of the world's leading universities. Yet, in some cases, in spite of their high level of education and extensive experience, I have seen these people lose sight of their vision of success, and become derailed and underperform in their work. This is a complex issue and there is no easy answer as to why this occurs. However, in many cases, I observed it was the individual's own behaviour that had let them down. They failed to regulate their own emotions, actions and the way in which they communicate with others. I have seen this happen within small and large organisations, from the most junior manager through to the most senior executive.

In his ground-breaking research into the field of emotional intelligence (EQ), Daniel Goleman identified that there was no causal link between high levels of intelligence (IQ) and emotional intelligence (EQ). Furthermore, he consistently found that EQ surpasses IQ as a more effective measure of sustained performance. This explains why on occasion intelligent people do stupid things; they fail to regulate their EQ. Goleman suggests that it is advantageous for people to develop higher levels of self-awareness and self-management, as well as social awareness and relationship skills.

Emotional intelligence is critical in the workplace given that some of the most common triggers for workplace conflict include lack of respect and appreciation, blame, and perceived imbalances in fairness. EQ plays a critical role in identifying issues and effectively navigating through these moments. I have witnessed conflict between individuals in the workplace – not as a result of intellectual inability but, rather, through lack of self-awareness, awareness of others, emotional imbalance and poor behaviour management skills.

Behavioural problems are further compounded when these same individuals are affected by increased levels of stress and pressure. What typically happens in the workplace when an individual's behaviour spirals out of control is that it causes relationship conflict, irrational decision making and decreasing performance levels. This is toxic for both the individual and their team. It directly affects the work they do and, if left unchecked, can have a negative impact on the organisation's culture.

As previously discussed, emotional intelligence (EQ) can be defined as an individual's level of self-awareness, awareness of others and the way in which they regulate their behaviour accordingly. Harvard theorist Howard Gardner has identified five categories of EQ:

1. Awareness of self and others.
2. Self-regulation of emotions.
3. Motivation, including drive to achieve, commitment, initiative and optimism.
4. Empathy (i.e. the ability to recognise how others feel).
5. Social skills, including good interpersonal skills.

We have already seen that EQ is a more influential factor in achieving success than IQ. Given that one of the major influences of EQ is self-awareness, it is critically important for you to develop an in-depth understanding of who you are (which includes the good, the bad and the ugly!). I cannot stress this point strongly enough; at all costs it is vital to 'get to know yourself' well. In other words, aim to discover what makes you, YOU. Develop your awareness of your strengths, weaknesses and how your behaviour affects others. Recognise how others perceive you and why you react to situations in the way that you do.

By developing your self-awareness, you will be in a much better position to understand what type of a working environment, job, leadership style and workplace culture suits your behavioural profile. This is important information which can further enhance your chances of success throughout your career. By building your personal data bank of self-awareness, you will be vastly better equipped to regulate your behaviour during periods of high stress and conflict that will inevitably occur during your career lifecycle.

Your brilliant career vision will become nothing more than an illusion if you don't make the effort to develop your self-awareness. Note to self: this process is a very long journey in itself and, to be brutally honest, it should be a lifelong quest. You should consider this as an opportunity to learn something new and exciting about yourself and others, but only if you choose to maintain an open mind. By adopting an attitude that embraces feedback and a willingness to learn from experience, you will be significantly better prepared to deal with the complexity of workplace dynamics and the hyper-change environment in which we live.

Having a good understanding of yourself is a skill that has the potential to 'keep on giving' until the day you die. Over the course of your career, this skill will help to open the door to new and exciting opportunities, as well as greatly improving your ability to communicate and engage with others. Additionally, developing your self-awareness will further help you to define your personal brand and your value proposition. Defining your personal brand goes beyond simply understanding what your strengths and weaknesses are; it involves understanding who you truly are.

Initially, developing your self-awareness can seem like a confronting and daunting process, but it is a critical part of the journey as you move forward toward your vision of success. It is a big piece of the puzzle that requires you to engage a range of strategies and tools. Making use of behavioural assessment tools is an excellent starting point and there are a vast number of options readily available in the market and online. That said, I would highly recommend you engage the support of a certified behavioural assessment practitioner, coach or organisational psychologist to assist you with this process.

If you are in the fortunate position whereby your company or leader already has a focus on self-development, they may also be willing to guide you in the right direction. If this is not an option, there are some excellent organisational psychologists and professional coaches who can assist you. Without doubt, this is one of the wisest investments you can make in your career! I have seen some amazing and inspiring outcomes from professional coaching intervention. However, research different options thoroughly as the relationship with your psychologist or coach has a direct influence on the results you are likely to achieve.

The sporting arena is an excellent example where an investment in coaching is highly regarded. The average career of a professional athlete is between five to seven years, and during those years, the majority of their training and competitive time is spent under the watchful eye of a coach. In this way, it is reasonable to assume that the process of coaching is greatly valued by high-performing athletes.

As most of us can expect to spend four decades of our lives working, it is madness not to engage a coach or mentor to support us in our career journey, particularly when career lifespans are likely to continue to become longer. Your coach and/or mentor are part of your support team so make sure you seek them out and then select them carefully.

While developing your self-awareness is important, in isolation it is not sufficient to ensure your success, although it certainly goes a long way towards helping you achieve your desired outcome. Identifying what you are truly passionate about and focusing your energy on what matters most are equally important. What are your strengths from a competency perspective? Do you enjoy bringing data to life, making numbers talk, connecting with others or creating something new? Regardless of the answer, linking your passions with what you actually do from a work perspective is an extremely powerful combination.

Take a moment to reflect without passing judgement. Think about the Rolling Stones rock band. Regardless of your generation or taste in music, they are a very powerful and recognisable brand – well, for most people – and even in their seventies, their passion is alive and well! Not only that but they have the necessary competencies to be world-class musicians. In their case, passion, competency and dare I say it, behaviours all aligned to ensure that they became one of the world's best and longest-playing rock bands of all time.

What are you truly passionate about? What are you good at? How self-aware are you really?

In order to answer these questions, you need to step back for a moment and reflect on where you have come from. You are the sum total of your DNA, upbringing, choices, life experience, environment and education. Each of these factors offers a wealth of information to help you understand what has shaped you and also to identify your strengths, weaknesses and, of course, what it is that you are truly passionate about.

Taking the time to reflect on your life experience provides you with an opportunity to identify the most vivid and enjoyable moments in your life, as well as those moments that most challenged you. What were those experiences? Where did they take place and what did you learn at the time? On the flip side, take another trip down memory lane and think of those moments that most challenged you. Once again, reflect upon what you learned at that time from those experiences.

Let's face it. We have all experienced both highs and lows in life. A permanent state of happiness is a worthy pursuit but it's not reality. Your life and career will be full of extreme highs and lows ... and everything in between.

To truly learn from any moment in your life – both good and bad – and move on with a greater level of knowledge and understanding, you must reflect on what took place at that time and understand how you processed the situation within your own mind. In some instances, you may also need the support of a trusted friend, family member or professional to help you work through a situation in order to reflect more deeply and ultimately to learn new information which will benefit you in the future.

The experiences you have in life provide great insight into who you are and how you have developed, as well as helping you understand how you might best utilise your skills in your future life and career. These same experiences also help you to identify development opportunities that will serve you well in both your career and life. Embrace these experiences as they will continue to shape who you are; they are part of your life and career journey. There is always significant learning to be had in any experience you have in your life.

Ok, let's now move on. Your educational experience, both formal and informal, will tell you something about what you enjoy and what you don't. Did you enjoy and excel at mathematics? Is developing an understanding of mathematics and its application to daily life or work something you wish to pursue further? Are you truly passionate about mathematics or is it something that you prefer to avoid at all cost?

Your formal education may tell you something about what you enjoyed at school or college which is useful information, but the results you achieved are certainly not a predictor of performance and success in your future career. Generally speaking, your past educational track record is not a reliable indicator of future performance outcomes.

Meet Michael

I remember speaking with a very good friend of mine – let's call him Michael to protect his true identity. At school, Michael staggered across the finishing line in mathematics. At best, he was a C-grade student in his early years but, later on in his life, he graduated with a Masters in Mathematics with a number of Distinctions. I asked him how this outcome had occurred. His reply was fascinating and not dissimilar to my own experience at school. According to Michael, 'It was not the case that I did not understand what was being taught. It was the way it was being taught that put me off. My maths teacher was often angry and when anyone in the class got something wrong, he generally made an example of them. I enjoyed numbers but I did not like my maths teacher. In fact, I was scared of him and that put me off mathematics all together. If I had not been encouraged by my parents to pursue my love of numbers I may not have even made it to university'.

When he first started at university, Michael was lucky enough to connect with a number of his university lecturers who were passionate about the subject of mathematics but also recognised Michael's abilities and encouraged him in his studies. Over time, he developed an amazing ability to review the financials of a business and very quickly identify how the business could optimise its performance from both an operational and financial perspective. This is a talent that Michael now leverages to his benefit and for the companies he consults for. But, most importantly, he enjoys his work immensely. It has become his passion and his philosophy is now: 'I enjoy numbers but I am passionate about the story they tell'.

The quality of your primary and secondary education and the interactions you had with your teachers during this period can certainly influence your choice of career and whether or not you go on to pursue higher education. In my opinion, the current school education system has a lot to answer for in terms of limiting the future potential and creativity of the next generation. Force-feeding children an education curriculum that does not permit free thought or recognise the individual ultimately pigeon holes students into rigid structures and stifles the creativity of these future leaders.

Some of the most successful people I'm aware of did not complete higher education. Rather, they decided to do what they enjoy most and pursued it with unrelenting passion, grit and single-minded determination. For example, Richard Branson and Bill Gates both dropped out of higher education. By his own admission, Branson is dyslexic and struggled to grasp the concept of gross and net profit from a financial perspective, yet he has been able to build a global empire. Yes, education is important but, in my opinion, experience, passion, drive and persistence matter more.

Think for a moment about those people who have influenced your life over the years. Who are they and what do you admire (or not admire) about them? What did you learn from your contact with them and how can you put this to good use? In your working life, if you're lucky you will have the chance to work with some amazing individuals and leaders. However, on occasion, you will meet others who will teach you more about what not to do as a leader as opposed to what you should do. Such is the reality of working life and as an experience this is perfectly ok. Learn from it, take what is good and then move on.

If you can learn to adopt the mindset that every life moment is an opportunity to learn and grow, you will never be in a position where you are wasting your time.

What matters most is that you learn from people in your life and the experiences you have and be grateful for them. Robert Emmons has conducted studies into the subject of gratitude and has identified that gratitude increases happiness and empathy, and reduces depression and aggression. What matters most is that we constantly strive to grow and learn from every situation in our lives. I have spoken to many people who have achieved a certain level of success in their life and they often say that they learn more from moments of adversity and challenge than from normal daily life dealing with the status quo. Above all, it is the mindset you adopt during these moments of adversity and challenge that will serve you well throughout your life.

I would like you to consider this question: before you started reading this book did you regularly set goals for yourself? If so, what were they? Did you achieve them or move closer towards them? If not, why was that the case? By thoughtfully and honestly reflecting on these questions, you will start to identify what might have prevented you from achieving your goals in the past. You may also identify what you have learned that will, in turn, allow you to refocus and commit to your future goals. This is an important reflection. If you have experienced blockages such as a loss of motivation, procrastination and lack of accountability, you need to understand why this happened in order to avoid repeating the same behaviour. This is not an easy step and on occasion it can be painful to look back. However, by doing so, you open the door to increasing your chances of achieving your goals in the future. Look for those patterns of behaviour that allowed you to progress towards your goals and made you feel happy, as well as igniting your passion. Be aware also of those patterns of behaviour that put you into a negative state and prevented you from achieving your goals.

As mentioned previously, we live in turbulent times. Therefore, in spite of the many life and career experiences you have had that have served you well up to this point, you should be aware that you will need to constantly adapt your skills, as well as your behaviours, to keep up with the current speed of change in the world. In other words, being adaptable and open to change are essential skills for you to cultivate and they can be improved if you are willing to commit to developing them.

In today's workforce, performance does matter and your performance reputation has an impact on your personal brand and will follow you wherever you go. Gaining a better understanding of your past and present will help you to plot a course for your future. It will also help you to understand what value you bring to the company you work for. Remember that good companies don't stand still. For this reason, you must be willing to adapt and stay ahead of the change curve, or run the risk of being left behind.

Reflection

1. Learning from the past is crucial to enhancing your chances of future success.

2. Developing greater self-awareness is 'mission critical' to sustained performance.

3. Identify your strengths in order to move closer and more quickly to your vision of success.

4. The difference between a winner and a true champion is not how often they win; it's what they do when they lose to then ensure that they will win the race another day, after day, after day.

5. Expect to fail … and to fail again. Understand that this is ok but learn from each failure so that you move closer towards success in future.

6. To increase your chances of success you will need to develop higher levels of motivation, confidence and self-belief. In addition, you need a plan that will help you to move towards your definition of success.

7. Understand that success comes through hard work and it is not a solo journey.

8. Identify what you are passionate about and ensure you are in a position to pursue it.

9. If you don't know who you are, you can bet no one else will either!

Chapter Seven

Building resilience

Exploration of our own minds is perhaps the last great frontier. Every journey is unique and has the potential to unlock unrealised potential. In this space we can all be great adventurers.

As I discussed in Chapter 4, it is important to reflect on your past in order to plan for your future. Hopefully, by now, you will have identified moments in your career journey that you did and didn't enjoy. You have also had the opportunity to reflect upon what you are truly passionate about. Conversely, you may have identified certain situations or moments that you would like to avoid in the future. Regardless of the outcome, this has been a useful exercise – particularly if you have been able to gain new knowledge and insight as a result of this process.

Taking time to gain a deeper understanding of who you are, what your strengths are and what motivates you will greatly assist you in finding direction in your career. As you work through this process, start to think about what you need to do in your current situation to enhance your performance and, most importantly, your enjoyment of your job. Additionally, you should start to think about what your next opportunity might be and how that could move you closer to your definition of success.

Your cognitive ability may (and I should stress – may) have an impact on your performance in certain situations throughout the course of your career. For example, verbal, numerical and abstract reasoning abilities vary from person to person. For this reason, someone who has a high level of numerical ability may be better suited to roles within financial services or engineering, as opposed to an individual who has a high level of verbal ability, who may be better suited to a role which relies on this particular cognitive skillset.

As you have discovered earlier in this book, your self-awareness and EQ are far greater determining factors in achieving success in the workplace than your cognitive ability. Likewise, your determination, motivation and ability to work hard are all important characteristics that will move you closer towards success.

Your mindset, which is often described as Attitude, within the workplace can be your greatest asset or liability and will always be the greatest single contributing factor to achieving sustained success.

Thankfully, your attitude is also one aspect of your mind that you can influence through the choices you make each day. Choosing a positive attitude means consciously adopting a solution-based approach as opposed to a problem-focused approach to your life, work and career. Doing this doesn't mean that you don't also consider the risks and challenges you may face in any given situation. In fact, risk assessment is an essential aspect of what you need to do to thrive in the workplace. However, you will greatly increase your chances of success if you develop the ability to direct your focus and energy to finding the solution with an open mind.

How you approach a challenging and stressful situation from a mindset perspective has a direct influence on the upshot of that situation. Your initial reaction will set the tone for the future outcome. In other words, do you adopt a problem-based approach or a solution-based approach to a situation? When you start to think 'solution' as opposed to 'problem', you will save time, generate creative ideas and move more quickly towards the ultimate goal of finding an answer to the challenges you face.

Research undertaken by the Mayo Clinic in 2007 found that positive thinking not only helps in managing stress but has other health benefits, including increased lifespan, a decrease in depression, an improved immune system response, better psychological and physical wellbeing, reduced risk of cardiovascular disease and improved capability to cope during periods of stress and hardship. It's true – if you change your attitude you can change your life!

Interestingly, when you start thinking about challenges from a solution-focused perspective you will also find that your motivation and enjoyment of the task at hand will increase greatly. Without doubt, today's workplace is a fast-paced, dynamic and competitive environment and tomorrow's is likely to be no different. Companies have a choice about who they employ and they will always choose someone with a positive attitude first.

Following on from the Global Financial Crisis, the recruitment market has seen a definite shift in terms of what is often described as the 'war on talent'. The reality is that the war on talent is now over and talent has won, with companies selecting the best talent available in the market. However, in comparison to the number of employment opportunities that currently exist, there are many more candidates than ever before in the market and competition for those roles is high. Offshore labor solutions, as well as the emergence of automation technology in the form of robotics will further increase competition levels. Part-time employment, periods of unemployment and contract work are set to become the norm.

Increased competition, technology and pressure to perform in the workplace from a competitive and performance perspective are the new reality. Understanding the dynamics of this environment is important but knowing how to manage the associated stress by building your resilience is key. Becoming more resilient will greatly assist you to improve your performance in the workplace and, hence, your chances of career success.

As an organisational psychologist, company director and executive coach with more than 30 years' experience, Kathryn McEwen has a particular interest in workplace resilience. She is the author of the book *Building Resilience at Work* and has developed a Resilience at Work toolkit (R@W Toolkit), as well as a Resilience at Work scale (R@W Scale) in conjunction with Dr Peter Winwood. In her research, McEwen explores the different elements of work resilience, including:

- Mastering stress
- Adapting to change
- Being proactive.

In her book, McEwen identifies seven key components of building resilience which include:

- *Authenticity:* Knowing and holding on to your personal values, deploying your strengths, and having a good level of emotional awareness and regulation.

- *Purpose:* Working in an area/industry that offers you purpose and a sense of belonging. Your work should also align with your core values and beliefs.

- *Adaptability:* Staying optimistic and keeping a solution-focus mindset when things go wrong. Reframing setbacks and minimising the impact of any negativity around you.

- *Self-care:* Creating work and life routines that help you to manage daily stressors. Working to create life-work balance and ensuring time for relaxation and recovery.

- *Support:* Seeking feedback, advice and support, including providing support readily to others.

- *Energy:* Maintaining a good level of physical fitness, having a healthy diet and getting adequate sleep.

- *Networks:* Developing and maintaining the personal and professional support networks you need at home and at work in order to perform well in your job.

Building your resilience should become a part of how you approach your career and life. Doing so will have a positive impact on your performance, your ability to manage stress and your balance and will assist you to achieve your goals.

Reflection

1. Learn to self-reflect in order to improve your performance.

2. A positive attitude will always win the day.

3. Adopt a solution-focused approach to your career and the significant challenges you face.

4. Develop your support network. Who is on your 'Team You'?

5. Building your resilience will help you to enjoy higher levels of performance, satisfaction, happiness and wellbeing.

Chapter Eight

Walking the high wire

The pursuit of your potential has no finish line but you must first commit to starting the race.

Life can be precarious at the best of times and your career will be no different. This is hardly surprising when you consider the number of different roles, responsibilities and variables that you will have to face and manage over the course of your lifetime. Yet, while life is precarious in nature, it is also full of opportunities and challenges. All in all, your life is precious and filled with endless possibilities. The more positive your mindset, the more possibilities you will be aware of in order to build a rich, fulfilling and meaningful career and life.

One of the most accurate descriptions I have come across regarding an individual's career is that it is like walking on a circus high wire while juggling. It can be incredibly exhilarating and it requires great skill to navigate from one side of the wire to the other. The risks are high but the rewards can be great. Falling is inevitable and a safety net is crucial. But it is what you do after a fall that makes all the difference.

Like life, your career has the potential to be filled with amazing opportunities and, similar to walking on a high wire, the workplace can be perilous if you fall. By preparing yourself well and developing self-awareness regarding the various components that shape who you are, I sincerely believe you will greatly enhance your chances of success. That's not to say that you will never stumble or fall; however, you will be more able to recover and, ultimately, to climb back up and continue.

From a career perspective, you need to understand that your career vision, goals and, ultimately, your choices will lead you in the direction that you want to go. However, you must constantly strive to improve your game and avoid stagnation at all cost. To do this successfully, it is important for you to find your own balance. I firmly believe that, in this age of the knowledge worker, a segmented approach to achieving a work/life balance is unrealistic because work itself has become such a large part of life.

Technology brings work into your home and there is now an increasing expectation from companies for you to be constantly connected in terms of your accessibility and responsiveness to email, instant messaging and other forms of communication. What this means is that your work crosses the line between your private life and your working life. The boundaries are often blurred and, in my opinion, this is likely to continue as technology and flexible work solutions evolve.

With this new reality in mind, it is important to strive to achieve an overall balance in your life as opposed to seeking to separate your work from your life. However, like the battery in your iPhone, you need to give yourself time to recharge. In addition, everyone needs to have down time and so you should consider scheduling a zero technology ban one hour before going to bed and, if possible, at least one day per week. Also, give yourself permission to have time away from technology during your working day and use this time to think, to verbally communicate with your colleagues. Remember, you manage the technology – don't allow technology to manage you.

When it comes to planning your career it is essential that you consider how to best balance your family, friends, interests, personal health and wellbeing, technology, finances and all that you value in life as part of your overall planning process.

Some questions you need to ask yourself are:

- What do you value most in your life?
- What are your short-, mid- and long-term priorities?
- What aspects of your current life do you want to carry into your future and what do you wish to let go?

Now is as good a time as any to reflect on these questions and to assess where you currently are in your life and career. Aim to pinpoint those aspects of your life that you find most rewarding, as well as those aspects that hold you back or prevent you from moving towards the life and the career you aspire to.

Try to be as objective as possible as you work through this process. Be open-minded and talk to those people in your life whom you both trust and respect. I have endeavored to include a range of topics here that I think will assist you in this process, but feel free to include any topic that you consider to be essential in your life. It is important to set boundaries as part of this process. Your boundaries ultimately define what you are prepared to accept and how far you are prepared to go, and are further influenced by your values. The boundaries that you set in your life and career will influence your goals, relationships and, to some extent, personal conduct and behavior. They form the safety net which will further enhance your resilience and reduce, but not completely cancel out, your risk of failure.

Take your thinking far beyond where you currently are in your life and dare to dream big.

Some more questions to consider include:

- What are your current career priorities and are they still relevant in your life?
- What do you need to stop, start and keep doing in your life to progress towards your career vision?
- In terms of your health and wellbeing – are you fit and able to cope with life and the challenges that inevitably lie ahead?
- How can you make your personal and professional relationships more fulfilling?
- Is your financial situation sustainable? What would you like to change and have you sought professional advice in order to build a financial plan that you find acceptable?
- In terms of your current job – are you still enjoying it and if not what could you do to change that?
- In terms of your personal and professional growth – are there new skills and experiences you would like to acquire? If so, what are they and what do you need to do to make this happen?

I have seen many examples first-hand of people who have not only reinvented their careers but also totally transformed their lives by having the courage to ask themselves questions they would not normally consider.

Meet Paul

Let me now provide a real working example of a coaching assignment I once undertook. For privacy reasons, I have altered this person's name to protect their identity. Paul made his money during the mining boom in Australia and when I say 'made his money', I mean that Paul was very wealthy. He had no boundaries regarding what he was prepared to accept in relation to his wealth. Enough was never enough for Paul and he continued to work hard – anything from 65 hours to 70 hours per week, plus the inevitable task of catching up with his emails on weekends. This scenario went on for some years. For Paul, this became his normal lifestyle; however, for his family it became unbearable. Paul had no plan and no vision of where he wanted to take his career or his life for that matter. His focus was solely on making money … and lots of it.

In the absence of a career vision supported by values, cracks in Paul's life started to appear just before the Global Financial Crisis. Paul started drinking as a way of coping with the stress in his life, most of which was caused by his pursuit of money and increasing debt levels as he followed the dream of more and bigger is better. A bigger car, a bigger house and more 'toys' in the driveway, including a sports car, boat and jet ski – there appeared to be no end to his thirst for 'stuff'. Paul had not established boundaries in either his career or life; he was living a life of excess based on the pursuit of money.

Paul's health started to suffer and he gained a lot of weight due to lack of exercise, poor diet and excessive alcohol and prescription drug consumption. His action plan was to work harder and so work harder he did. While he was away on a business trip, his wife walked out on him, along with his two beautiful children, and she later filed for divorce. The Global Financial Crisis hit and Paul's world continued to fall apart. He lost his job, his house, all of his 'toys' and cash wealth. Yes, that's right – he lost everything that he valued!

I spoke to Paul on the phone and he expressed an interest in engaging in coaching. He invited me to meet him for a coffee and when we first met we sat quietly for some time drinking our coffee. Paul was broken and could not even afford to pay for his coffee, let alone the coaching sessions with me. After a period of silence, I looked at him and smiled. 'So what's the plan, Paul?' I said. His reply was interesting. 'All I know is that what got me here will not take me to where I need to be'. Paul then went on to talk about his obsession with money and how it had taken over his life.

However, money was no longer a priority to him – not because he did not have any but because his health problems had become an even bigger issue for him. He had developed severe anxiety compounded by a sleep disorder. On top of this, he had been diagnosed with depression. As Paul said, 'The rise and fall of Paul allowed me to evaluate what my real priorities were. My focus in life has now shifted from money to my health and my children'. Paul started to link his work with his life priorities, and he identified what he needed to stop, start and keep doing. Paul began to exercise and moderate both his diet and alcohol intake.

Paul also realised that the people in his life, with the exception of his family, were also obsessed with money and they quickly vanished when he lost his job and wealth. He needed to rebuild his friendship base and create 'Team Paul' to help him get to where he wanted to be.

He also decided that he needed to obtain new knowledge to reinvent his career and so, in his forties, went back to tertiary study. By asking himself the right questions and by focusing on his health, family and circle of close friends who truly cared about him, Paul started to rebuild his life. Likewise, by setting goals that were realistic and achievable, Paul began to enjoy the satisfaction of achieving, but this time with a strong sense of purpose and boundaries. Paul's health improved as he continued to exercise and moderate his diet and lifestyle. He was also able to regularly see his children and play an active role as a loving and engaged father.

Paul recently completed his university studies at a PhD level and is now a financial advisor and consultant. Yes, that's right! Paul now helps other people to become wealthy. He is very good at it and his services are in high demand. Based on his own experience, he understands how to make money but, most importantly, he now knows how to keep it. Despite his job, Paul is not focused on money at all. When he speaks with his clients for the first time, he asks them these questions: 'What do you value most in life?' and 'What is your definition of a good life as opposed to a successful life?' If their response is money, Paul talks about his own journey and insights. Paul has discovered the answer to the 'Why?' in his career and life. His purpose is now to help others avoid falling into the same trap he did.

Reflection

1. Your daily work and career will present many challenges. In order to prepare yourself for those challenges it is important to understand where you are now in terms of your work and life in order to make positive changes and plan for the future.

2. Both your career and life involve risk. Accept this fact and do all you can to ensure you have a safety net and support network around you.

3. Boundaries are important. Ultimately they reflect what we are prepared to accept in all aspects of our life.

4. By creating a career vision with a higher purpose and honestly exploring the question of 'Why you do what you do?', you will feel a greater level of engagement and satisfaction with your work. When reflecting on this point, think about the legacy you would like to leave behind and, ultimately, how you would like to be remembered.

Chapter Nine

Network matters

**In order to become interesting to others
we must first become interested.**

Success at any level is never a solo journey. As with all great adventures, there is usually an amazing team behind the scenes. I remember one particular conference I attended in which Tom Peters was the keynote speaker. Tom is well-known for his edgy, 'out of the park' business thinking and forthright quotes. However, on this occasion, there was one in particular comment he made that has stuck with me to this very day. 'You are who you eat your lunch with'. It was a show-stopper; the room went silent before the inevitable laughter kicked in.

Despite the entertainment value of this statement; for me there was a far deeper meaning to what Peters had said. Research suggests that the most important relationships for children (other than their parents) are within their peer group. These relationships influence your perspective on life, the choices you make, your behavior and so much more – as do the role models you look up to.

In the workplace, job satisfaction is significantly influenced by the relationships you have with those people you work with. Your colleagues at every level and the relationship you have with your boss certainly have an important impact on you in terms of their influence on your mindset, motivation and well-being.

You may have read and heard the phrase: People don't leave companies. Instead, they leave their boss.' But they also leave the people they work with if those relationships are dysfunctional. If you're not happy with the relationships you have at work and you continue to stay, you will not perform to your full potential and, in all likelihood, you will eventually end up leaving the company. The quality of your working relationships not only affects your overall satisfaction in terms of the view you have about the company you work for. I also believe they greatly influence your engagement and, ultimately, your performance levels in the workplace.

In recent years, a significant amount of research has been undertaken regarding the link between workplace relationships and employee engagement – perhaps most notably is by the Gallup Organisation. From my own experience, I have witnessed first-hand the impact this link can have on an employee's performance, resulting in professional disharmony between colleagues and a subsequent negative spillover effect on the team.

If left unchecked, dysfunctional relationships in the workplace can further intensify and spread to the point where they have a destructive impact on a company's culture and damage its brand reputation beyond repair. To an even greater extent, once this negativity has infiltrated a company's culture, it has the potential to be very detrimental to employee turnover, productivity, service delivery and, ultimately, bottom-line performance. Relationships matter and the quality of those relationships matter even more.

Without doubt, the relationships or network you maintain at a professional level are 'mission critical' to your future career success and have a significant influence on your personal brand reputation. One of the best definitions of personal brand that I have seen comes from Jeff Bezos, the founder of Amazon: *'Personal brand is what people say about you when you leave the room.'*

Ultimately, your personal brand is your reputation and is also influenced by the company you keep. With this last point in mind, your approach to networking should be undertaken with purpose. Your professional network is a very precious database and, like all databases, it needs to be well managed to ensure that it is current and relevant to where you are in your career at any given time.

There is a range of tools available that you can leverage to assist you with your networking efforts. Your resume or curriculum vitae (or CV as it is more commonly known) is the starting point and should always be up-to-date. It should be supported by a succinct, eye-catching career biography or summary. That includes your aspirations which can be used as a catalyst when you introduce yourself with your next opportunity in mind, as well as being reflective of your personal brand.

The advent of LinkedIn and other professional online networking platforms means that the content of your resume and online profile should be seamless. The content should be concise and ultimately measurable in terms of your achievements and the experience you have gained, as well as being supported with examples of specific achievements that can be further elaborated on when you are exploring new opportunities.

Your CV represents many aspects of who you are and what you have achieved, including your career journey to date, life experience, aspirations, interests, skillset and the overall value proposition you offer to your future employer. It also provides a much deeper insight into your personal brand. Given its importance and what it says about you, be sure you keep your CV 'real' and be careful not to over promise. At the same time, do not be overly modest and undersell yourself in terms of your experience, capabilities and achievements. All in all, it's a fine balance.

Your career vision needs to become clear in your mind's eye and you must be able to eloquently articulate it. When speaking with your manager about a promotion or to your next prospective employer for that dream job, you must be able to clearly present your career vision and the value that you offer.

Many people find it a challenge to sell themselves effectively in a job interview. Yet, if you don't sell yourself you can be sure no one else will. Your pitch needs to be authentic, succinct and must have impact. If the chance arises and you come in to contact with an individual or group who can help you to get where you want to go, you need to be able to sell yourself, and ultimately promote the strength of your personal brand. For maximum impact, you should be able to fully engage your prospective employer within the shortest timeframe possible and convince them that you are the hottest candidate on the market and that they would be foolish to look elsewhere.

If this concept makes you squirm in your seat, let me reiterate again that if you don't develop the confidence and self-belief to sell yourself and your abilities, I can assure you no one else will! It is not a case of putting yourself on center stage and screaming at the top of your voice, 'Hey, look at me! I'm simply amazing!' In a tight and competitive employment market where jobs are scarce you can bet that the number of people applying for work will continue to exponentially increase. It is not a matter of overselling yourself. Instead, it involves pitching yourself at the right level based on the opportunity at hand to ensure that you secure that next promotion or job opportunity that will move you in the right direction in terms of your career journey.

Your business card still matters! No, I am not talking about the good old-fashioned gold-emblazoned business card proudly wielded by the Baby Boomer generation. I am referring to your overall online presence which acts as the new business card. Your online presence – the posts and photos you upload to Instagram, Facebook, Twitter, LinkedIn and any other platform you choose to use – says volumes about you. Like it or not, it also provides another quick point of reference for those people you meet to form and shape their opinion of you.

Like your CV, your online presence should have an impact and reflect your personal brand and the value that you 'bring to the table'. Networking opportunities are no longer limited to career expos, industry events and company conferences. Thanks to the Web, networking is global and a 24 x 7 opportunity.

As for the traditional business card, it is no longer as relevant as it once was. Nevertheless, if your prospective new boss presents you with their own business card, returning the favor will be looked upon favorably, particularly if he or she is a Baby Boomer. Therefore, I suggest you keep your stock of business cards at the ready whenever networking opportunities arise. It's always an awkward moment when you meet someone for the first time in a formal business setting if you spend the first minute fumbling for a business card that you obviously don't have only to conclude the process with, 'I'm sorry

I seem to be all out of my business cards' or 'I am sorry they are at the printers'. It's equivalent to 'the dog ate my homework' in terms of an excuse.

In business in particular (and some people would say in society in general), we have perfected the art of talking at each other in an effort to drive our own personal or professional agenda. Often when people are not speaking, rather than truly listening they are preparing their next onslaught of verbiage to ensure their opinion is aired. And I stress this point of airing their opinion because more often than not it falls well short of being heard. By taking the time to truly understand others, you create a platform of goodwill upon which to start a meaningful dialogue. You also potentially generate an interest from the other person to engage and better understand your perspective.

Your networking efforts should not only have purpose but should also have clear objectives. Just because you have over 500 LinkedIn contacts does not mean they will further your cause or be a supporter of Brand You. If your intention is to transition your career from accounting to sales, you will need a totally different network to the one you currently have. Your network should include those people you work with who are high performers, as well as professional groups, mentors and company sites or individuals you aspire to work with. Networking opportunities should be explored both in person and online. Likewise, you should review your network on a regular basis.

Reflection

1. Seek out those people who inspire you and connect with them.

2. Network with those individuals who have achieved great things and have experience within your area of interest.

3. Create an exclusive network and don't focus on volume. Less is more and quality matters.

4. Collaborate and partner with people who are able to think in a way that is both innovative and entrepreneurial.

5. Quirky is good as often these people are the most creative.

6. Status quo provides consistency but creativity fuels change and innovation. Ensure your network includes a rich blend of people who bring a wide variety of skills and experience.

Chapter Ten

Seek wise counsel

The achievement of greatness is never a solo journey.

Although an extremely worthwhile investment, working with a professional business coach can be out of reach for many people due to the associated costs. Of course, there are other alternatives that can be as equally powerful in terms of both professional and personal development. Aligning yourself with those people who have a greater level of experience and have achieved measurable success can certainly provide you with greater insight and new learning.

Wise counsel can take such forms as formal and informal mentoring relationships – both of which can be extremely beneficial. Mentoring offers the opportunity to grow and develop in many ways, including how to manage change, career mapping, leadership development, project management, career transition and building greater levels of self-awareness. In addition, it can help you to gain a deeper insight and understanding of organisational politics, which is perhaps the most challenging area of all to manage, regardless of what stage you are in your career.

Organisational politics are a direct outcome of the personalities and leadership behaviours that exist within the company and are further shaped by the company's hierarchy, power dynamics, ambition and self-interest. Furthermore, internal politics shape the culture of companies, setting the standard in terms of acceptable behavior and even having an influence on the language used within that company. It is a complex subject but it is one that is certainly important to develop an understanding of.

In my opinion, managing office politics really comes down to a few key points:

- *Understanding*: Build your understanding of the politics that exist within your workplace. This is the starting point for developing your awareness of 'who is who in the zoo', including their level of authority, influence and self-interest, and it will assist you in assembling the political jigsaw puzzle. Be aware that this may take some time, particularly in terms of understanding the self-interest and true motivations of others. There can be many layers involved and you may never fully understand them.

- *Focus*: By maintaining your focus on what it is that you are required to do in your role, as a team and ultimately what the company is trying to achieve, you are more likely to avoid being drawn into political conflict.

- *Circle of influence*: This concept has been around for quite some time and, in relation to the workplace, it involves focusing on what and who you can influence as opposed to those situations and individuals you cannot. Once you have identified those issues i.e. those situations or individuals you cannot influence), it is important to simply let them go as they will only drain your energy and motivation and, ultimately, prevent you from focusing on what you can influence.

- *Remain neutral*: Whenever a political situation arises, don't be drawn into debate as to which side is right or wrong. Instead, focus once again on what you and the company are trying to achieve and what is in the best interests of the company. This is the high ground that will move the discussion towards a solution.

- *Don't take it personally*: The workplace can be a high-pressure environment in which many different individuals and personality styles are brought together under one roof. This reality, in combination with the pressure to perform, tight deadlines, budgets and competing priorities, has a direct impact on behavior. It's not personal unless you allow it to become so.

- *Listen first*: This is always a useful starting point. To quote Stephen Covey: 'Seek first to understand before being understood'. Adopting this approach will help you, particularly in situations where conflict or a difference of opinion exists.

- *Adopt a solution-focused mindset*: In a politically-charged environment or discussion it is easy to become caught up in power plays or self-interest that exists. Focus on the solution first. Why are we here? What are we trying to achieve and what is the best outcome for the business?

By taking these seven points on-board you will be in a good position to navigate through organisational politics. However, when the pressure is on it can be easy to be drawn into political debate. Aligning yourself with a mentor who understands the culture and the politics that exist within your place of work will further help you manage this aspect of your working life.

The depth and complexity of the topics discussed with your mentor very much depends on the openness of the relationship and the willingness of both parties to explore the topics that matter most. In addition, the level of trust and the agreed boundaries of the relationship will have a direct influence not only on the topics discussed but also the potential outcomes of the mentoring relationship.

In the age of the knowledge worker, mentoring is widely regarded as one of the most effective learning and developmental interventions. It has application in a wide and increasing range of industries such as the finance sector, education, tourism and the armed services. Mentoring can be deployed to support the onboarding of new employees, succession planning and talent development initiatives. Seeking wise counsel in the form of an experienced mentor has the potential to not only improve your performance in your current role but also to provide a clearer sense of direction for your future career.

Career development can take many different forms. Sometimes it may come from the most unlikely of sources; someone completely separate from your place of work, but who is an individual whom you both trust and respect. What is important is that you seek out these people – after first ensuring that they have the ability to be objective and non-judgmental, and they have the courage to challenge your thinking and decision-making with your best interests at heart. Unfortunately, these relationships are all too rare in both life and the workplace, so when you do find them make sure you nurture and protect them.

Another valuable source of guidance and support might take the form of a subject matter expert who can offer a rich source of information in their given field of expertise, as well as providing insight and knowledge that can be extremely beneficial depending on your specific needs. These individuals do not necessarily have to be a coach or mentor, but they should be knowledgeable in their field of expertise. Ultimately, they should provide you with an opportunity to fill a knowledge gap that you currently lack.

Reflection

1. It is critical that you build relationships with those individuals who are genuinely interested in your personal and professional development and have a sincere desire to see you succeed.

2. Winners attract winners. Set the bar high when it comes to goal setting which, in turn, will push you to your limits. As the saying goes: 'You are who you eat your lunch with'. Therefore, make sure that you seek out those people who are successful or who aspire to achieve great things.

3. Making the effort to attend conferences, seminars and professional development events will not only offer you new learning, but also provide high-quality network opportunities.

4. Surround yourself with people who are high performers, motivated and truly passionate about what they do.

Chapter Eleven

Make it happen

Definition of success: To have the freedom to choose what you would like to achieve and then to achieve it.

For many of you, making things happen or turning your best intentions into reality is often the most difficult step in any personal transformation process. Making things happen is all about first acknowledging the need to change, committing to the goals you have set and then taking action. Converting your good intentions into tangible outcomes is difficult at the best of times, but in a fast-paced work environment it can be even more difficult. Simply finding time to step off the 'treadmill of life' can be challenging enough in itself. Being creatures of habit, we continually run the risk of falling into routine and complacency, which are the greatest enemies of personal and professional growth.

Given the pressures of daily life and the impact this has on your available time, it is important for you to develop a career plan that is concise, measurable and no more than one page long. Most importantly, you must accept that you (and only you) are accountable for your progress towards the goals you have set yourself. Yes, that's right – you are accountable for your actions! You hold the key to the decisions you make. Accepting and taking responsibility for your actions is powerful in terms of establishing the right mindset to allow change to occur. It is also extremely empowering when you recognise that you are in charge of your career and your life journey: a realisation that can be likened to that of a hunter rather than the hunted.

The most sophisticated career plan is meaningless unless you take time to develop a positive mindset that will allow you to commit to and go after what it is you want to achieve. As for the plan itself, ultimately it should provide a structured pathway, as well as a point of reference in terms of what you should be doing and when it should be achieved. More specifically, it will help to ensure you are accountable for your own actions. The plan should be specific and include dates linked to the goals you have set yourself. Your goals should be big, bold and ambitious since this represents your opportunity to push yourself from where you currently are to where you want to be in the future.

Your plan should include your career vision as part of an overriding strategy and direction. The next essential step involves creating well-crafted goals that move you towards that vision. These could include a role change within your current place of work or to another company all together.

There is a significant amount of research which explores the importance of developing goals that are measurable, attainable and have a set timeframe. However, the bottom line is that your goals should be clear and measurable in terms of what you aspire to achieve and when you plan to complete that goal. In addition to establishing well-defined goals, be sure that you include check points along the way that will ultimately progress you towards each goal. For example, if your ultimate goal is to transition into a new employment opportunity, you could allocate three hours per week to researching companies online within your chosen professional field.

An additional target could be to attend two networking events per month to further increase your chances of moving into your next role or to simply expand your professional network. Regardless, you will need to get busy and ensure that both your goals and check points are interlinked and relevant. Your plan should also include regular touch points with your support network, coach or mentor in order to discuss the challenges you are facing. Identify who within your support network is best positioned to assist you with each goal and then put them to work ... in the nicest possible way! In other words, you should ensure you discuss your goals with them and ask for their feedback and insights.

Most importantly, have the courage to share your plan with those individuals you trust. If you commit both internally and externally to your goals there is a far greater chance that you will actually achieve what you have set out to do. In other words, what you commit to internally establishes a winning mindset and what you proclaim externally creates accountability, drive and healthy pressure to do what you have said you wanted to achieve. Commit to physically recording your goals on your computer or on paper. Your career plan should be a visual tool that is displayed where you can see it every day.

Your career plan is a dynamic document that should be reviewed on a regular basis. Goals and supporting actions may need to be changed or adapted as new information, or unexpected challenges and opportunities arise. This is absolutely normal and in reality is an essential part of any effective planning process.

Both your life and your career represent wonderful opportunities to accomplish great things so ensure that you take time to celebrate the achievement of your goals along the way. If you have set your goals high they will be worthwhile to applaud and remember – small wins count. The celebration represents a great form of motivation. Whenever an athlete achieves a personal best they not only celebrate, but, guess what … they set the bar even higher for themselves.

So far we have explored a process that has the potential to both identify your next opportunity and also to catapult your career on a completely different trajectory to the one you are currently on. When viewed in isolation, the process itself seems quite simple: you need to take the time to assess your past and who you are, as well as start to set goals which will ultimately progress you towards your career vision.

I have mentioned previously that your career journey is not a solo undertaking but, rather, a journey that will be greatly enriched by seeking help from others who are genuinely interested in seeing you succeed. Work is only tedious if you choose to make it so. The fact is if you choose to adopt the right mindset and establish a clear vision of what you would like to achieve from your career, it will become a source of motivation and great satisfaction for you. What is important to note in the age of the 'knowledge worker' is that, within reason, you are blessed with the ability to choose what direction your career will take. All you have to do is to actually make a decision about what that direction will be and then commit to it.

Reflection

1. Rapidly developing technology and work-force globalisation will continue to have an impact on how and where you work, as well as what type of work will be available to you.

2. It is important to identify what the emerging workplace trends are to ensure that you can adapt, maintain relevancy and seize opportunities as they become available.

3. Career planning is a process of turning goals into reality.

4. Your plan should be linked to your career vision and the goals that you set yourself should be supported by measurable activities that move you closer to that vision, one step at a time.

5. Be sure to build some flexibility into your plan. Failure is useful to your growth so make sure that you actively take risks.

6. You are accountable for your career journey and the achievement of goals and actions you set.

7. Build in checkpoints to ensure you are heading in the right direction and then review them regularly.

8. Celebrate success, regardless of how small it may be.

Chapter Twelve

Think like an entreprenuer

**Leadership + empowerment
= accountability.**

Applying the mindset of an entrepreneur in terms of how you view your job and career may be a new concept for many of you. However, I believe it is critical to apply such a mindset if you are going to truly engage with your work and add value to the company you are employed by. Not only does this approach make your job more interesting, it also has a dramatic impact on how you view the company you work for, the decisions you make and the overall effort you put into your work. As a mindset, it has the potential to have a positive influence on your performance and the satisfaction you obtain from work itself.

A successful and long-lasting career will not be a reality for those individuals who merely wish to exist in their place of work; to clock in and clock out as it were. The 'lion's share' will go to those individuals who truly embrace their work, take charge of their careers and regard the company they work for as if it were their own.

The reality is that both business owners and leadership within companies will reward those individuals and teams who view the business through their eyes. Company structures are becoming flatter and the focus is moving away from improvements in pure profit and process to optimising both the employee and customer experience at every level within the business, regardless of industry. That does not mean that process is not important and profit is no longer relevant. Of course they are. However, like lights in a building, these two variables simply need to be present. On occasion, it may be necessary to change a globe or two and rewire the building but, ultimately, the lights just have to work. Process improvement alone will not leverage the potential of a workforce (or a company for that matter) and focus on profit alone does little to motivate and engage workers. People matter and it is the people, including their level of engagement, focus and their leadership qualities, that make the difference.

Visionary leaders recognise that ultimately their people need to feel empowered to make decisions at every level within the business: empowered to make decisions in the best interests of the business, as well as empowered to act with the customer in mind at all times. From an employee's perspective, the resulting impact of this is that both now and in the future there will be more opportunity than ever before to have a direct influence actively and tangibly on the direction of a company.

The emergence of project teams that are responsible for concentrating on initiatives designed to positively shift the focus of a business will increase significantly in the future. Moreover, the future employee profile will consist of individuals who are:

- Curious.
- Innovative and entrepreneurial.
- Able to look at their company from the outside in.
- Agile and flexible in terms of reacting to change.
- Have an open mindset and be willing to learn.
- Resilient.

- Expect to fail but be able to quickly move on to success.

In the future, companies will need to develop cultures that:

- Focus on creating an entrepreneurial culture as a priority.
- Reward risk and innovation.
- Are mindful of the social impact they have.
- Recruit and celebrate a diverse workforce.
- Give up control to gain influence and empower their workforce.
- Be prepared to fail … and to fail again.
- Focus on the wellbeing of their workforce and build resilience.
- Interview prospective employees for EQ.
- Develop an open mindset as part of their leadership culture.
- Align their people with their customer strategy.

Think for a moment about a situation in which you worked for a company (either small or large) where the leadership failed to empower their workforce. What impact did that have on staff morale?

When leaders fail to empower their workforce they create a culture of stagnation.

Teams and individual employees do not take responsibility for their own actions. Rather, they wait for approval instead of moving swiftly to find the solution themselves. The decision-making process slows down and employees become demotivated and disengaged.

When you start to think like an entrepreneur, you should be prepared to accept greater levels of responsibility and accountability way beyond the actual framework of your job description. Plan, take action and make decisions with the company's future and performance in mind – not simply from the perspective of your own role and the department you work for.

Once you commit to shifting your mindset from that of employee to entrepreneur, you can start to ask yourself some questions that will in turn have a positive impact on the business. Most importantly, it will improve your performance in your role within the company you work for. The positive outcome of this shift in thinking is that you will gain heightened satisfaction from your work, including the contribution you make and the value you bring to your organisation. That's right – your personal brand worth and reputation will also increase exponentially!

At this point, you should ask yourself:

- What actions can you take to better serve the company, customer and the team you lead and/or work for? Yes, that's right – 'work for'. Leadership and teamwork is ultimately about serving others, not yourself.

- What innovations would help your company not only 'out punch' but 'knock out' the competition?

- What revenue-generating opportunities and cost-saving initiatives would you implement if it were your company?

All of your decisions and actions should be executed with an entrepreneur's mindset. With this change in perspective comes a greater sense of freedom and empowerment. The conversations that you have in the workplace will change for the better and you will inevitably engage with the business at a different level.

In the future, companies will recruit talent with this entrepreneur's mindset as a prerequisite. Consequently, if you can develop and apply it now, you will not only improve your performance but also ultimately increase your employability and the number of opportunities that will be available to you in the future. So why wait? It's simply a matter of making a conscious decision and stepping up to the plate.

As mentioned earlier, in my opinion, as you become more empowered, you will also become more accountable for your actions. If accountability is something you struggle with – or even worse, avoid or deflect – you will find it very difficult to transition to the mindset of an entrepreneur. Effective leaders are accountable, pure and simple. They understand that the buck stops with them. Being accountable for your actions can also have a very positive impact on your performance as it means that you are responsible for any mistakes you make, as well as the successes you achieve. Learn to view failures as learning opportunities and you will become less fearful of accepting responsibility.

As your performance improves so too does the value that you bring to the company you work for and the team that you work with. Ideally, you should aim to bring value beyond what your salary costs the business. As a concept, this allows you to present a compelling business case to your current or future company that you bring something more to the negotiation table than your good intentions, experience and aspirations. In other words, you are able to show that you add real value to any organisation you choose to join.

Of course, your experience is both important and of value; however, experience alone will not 'cut it' in business, today or tomorrow. If your experience is no longer relevant it will ultimately affect your brand value and result in your eventual departure from a company. Experience adds credibility to your personal brand, but it is essential that you can apply your experience in a way that converts to tangible and profitable outcomes for the company you work for. With this concept firmly in mind, ask yourself:

- What value do you bring to the company you work for?
- How can you increase the value you bring to the business?

The long-held belief of a 'job for life' is no longer reality! Employment tenures are becoming shorter – on average, just over three years. Contract and part-time employment opportunities are increasing and more companies are looking to 'offshore' jobs to reduce payroll costs. Marking time in your current role without adding real value to your employer is not an option. Your length of service in a company counts for little unless you are adding value through the work you do.

In my opinion, length of service rarely equates with excellence in performance. In fact, over the years, I have observed many instances where those people who have served the longest often produce the least results. Top talent moves rapidly either within the company they work for or they take their personal brand offering to the competition.

Stagnation kills motivation, and creates complacency and routine. Of course, you are on dangerous ground if you become stagnant in your role as your colleagues and the leadership within your company will clearly pick up on it. More importantly, you run the risk of becoming redundant and, at the very least, endanger the progress of your personal brand and growth.

Performance does matter! If you fully embrace this idea, it will potentially allow you to step up to the challenge and demand more of yourself in your career. Avoid it at your peril as the harsh reality of today's workplace is that you are as good as your last email, meeting or project launch. Adding value and building your personal brand proposition need to be front and center of your mind. You need to become a valued and irreplaceable resource within your company. Strive to develop a reputation as the 'go-to person' in your company; someone who gets the job done!

Meet Carol

Carol could be described as being a Millennial. In other words, she is someone born between 1982 – 2007, who grew up surrounded by technology and electronics. As a group, Millennials are a generation that is connected online and very comfortable with using various social media platforms.

Carol is tolerant of differences, confident, lives in the moment and is more optimistic about the future than previous generations. She sends an average of 50 texts daily and spends a large percentage of her free time online. Balance in her life matters and she is less likely to put up with an unpleasant work environment than previous generations. Carol is concerned about social issues and fairness in all aspects of life.

From a career perspective, she expects instant career progression and direct access to her boss. She is efficient, adaptable and open to working both remotely and globally. She has a tendency to switch from one thing to the next and multi-tasks throughout her day. Carol is good at research and is confident about jumping in and giving things a go. She wants to be included on high-profile projects and expects to be asked her opinion. She also expects opportunity to knock on her door. She is comfortable working for more than one company at a time and wants to be well paid and promoted quickly during the early stages of her career. Carol is representative of the future of the workforce within companies.

Reflection

1. Having lived through the age of 'cash is king', we are now moving into the age of the 'customer rules'. Yes, cash is still important; however, if your company does not have an eye on the customer, the cash will very quickly dry up!

2. LOVE your customers, regardless of who they are.

3. Developing a mindset of service in all that you do is critical to your career success.

4. Adopt an entrepreneur's mindset to increase your motivation, career satisfaction and brand value.

Chapter Thirteen

Beyond the customer

In today's hyper-competitive market the quality of the employee experience and the customer experience will determine those companies which thrive as opposed to those that merely survive.

In this age of the 'knowledge worker', the 'customer is king'. Therefore, companies should focus on enhancing the customer experience at every touch point within their business as a matter of priority. This is without doubt 'mission critical' for any business. However, it is essential to note that there is a clear link between employee experience, employee engagement and the ability to create an optimal customer experience. This is an important point because, in order to achieve your full potential in your career, you must first understand this connection. Secondly, you must ensure that you choose the company you want to work for very carefully.

A good measure of the quality of any company is their employee experience, which equates to the moment a new employee walks into the company to the day they eventually leave. With this in mind, it is apparent that it is pointless to pour resources into complex and costly customer-focused initiatives if your business has a poor employee experience that ultimately results in a disengaged workforce.

Stay with me and let's explore this concept a little further. It is a well-researched fact that high levels of employee engagement create even higher levels of customer satisfaction and retention. The employee experience ultimately influences employee engagement, which in turn has a direct positive spill-over effect on the customer experience and retention of both employees and customers.

So what is the employee experience? Simply put, it's what happens when a potential or existing employee interacts with the company, regardless of what that touch point is. It starts with the moment they first come into contact with the company. Typically, this is the application process and everything in between. It is further influenced by the culture, values and quality of leadership within the company.

High-performing companies ensure that their employee experience is optimal and that their workforce is engaged. They develop a clear and compelling vision, foster a positive culture and encourage personal development within their workforce. Leadership is actively involved in ensuring the employee experience is 'best in class' and they listen to their people.

You should seek to align yourself with a company that is employee-focused and values a high-quality employee experience as part of their company culture. In addition, it is important that the company ensures they take a service-based approach to recruitment and actively promote their employer brand in line with a positive workplace culture.

The company's onboarding program should be comprehensive and take into account the needs of their new arrivals. They should be mindful that, as with any relationship, the first impression a new employee has of a company is a lasting one. First impressions count and have a direct impact on employee engagement and employee retention. It is the first 90 days that matter most; however, consistency is equally important. So ensure that you do your due diligence and research your next company properly.

Be sure to ask them about their on-boarding program and what it entails for new employees.

Some additional questions you should be asking include:

- What is being said about the company online?
- What are they doing to attract the right people?
- What benefits do they provide to their workforce?
- What sort of recognition programs do they offer?
- What are employees who work for the company saying about it to others?

Reflection

1. When Day One arrives and you start working for your new company, ask yourself: what time and effort did they invest in you to ensure your arrival into the company was exceptional?

2. First impressions count. So if that impression is a positive one, it will greatly influence your engagement, performance and commitment to that company.

3. Your career is precious and your experience as an employee will shape your perception of business life and ultimately how you view work.

4. Companies that create an exceptional employee experience will greatly enhance their chances of delighting their customers.

Conclusion

Thankfully, my career journey is not over and I am extremely excited about what future opportunities are ahead for me. However, the time has come for you to apply the learning you have obtained from this book. Take your time to truly reflect on where you are now in your career before thinking about where you want to take it in the future.

In today's workplaces, performance does matter and, as discussed throughout this book, the work environment itself can be very challenging. At the same time, it can offer amazing opportunities, as well as being a great source of meaning in your life. In my opinion, the opportunity to have meaningful work to do and to be able to carve out a career is truly a gift in the age of the knowledge worker. And, let's face it – the alternative is not particularly appealing.

Work itself offers many opportunities and, over the course of your career lifetime, can give you the opportunity to create a positive and lasting legacy. The nature of work is changing due to the ever increasing presence of technology, more flexible workplace solutions and the shifting dynamics of globalisation. In addition, the emergence of a 'gig'-based work culture provides the opportunity to be your own CEO; the prospects are endless depending on how you view your career and the opportunities that today's workplace provides.

My personal vision is to be able to achieve my potential by helping to release the potential in others. In pursuing this vision, I have been fortunate to have worked and travelled all over the world and still continue to do so, both professionally and privately. This in itself is a wonderful gift that I am extremely grateful for. That said, one of the most challenging aspects of any career journey is to define a personal vision of success and then to link that with your career aspirations.

The western education system and the workplace does little to prepare us for this experience. In fact, from the moment you enter the workforce you are expected to achieve and get things done. Over time, if you're lucky (and as a direct outcome of your own learning) you will have a better understanding of the importance of goals and the value of having a career and life vision. If you are fortunate enough to receive coaching, mentoring or higher level education, you then understand the wisdom of developing your self-awareness and emotional intelligence. Finally, you may start to understand the importance of linking what you do with a higher purpose, such as making a contribution beyond yourself as you move into the senior years of your working life.

I sincerely believe that when planning your career, it is critical to 'flip' this approach on its head. The elements are right but the order is wrong. In order to build a sustainable and successful career, the starting point should be self-awareness, including awareness of your behaviours and competencies. Taking time to develop your emotional intelligence will also greatly support this process. As a next step, the development of a career vision is a key driver in giving you direction in your career. When connected with measurable goals and actions that can be linked to your career vision, this strategy will continue to guide you on your journey through the inevitable highs and lows of your career. Finally, once you have achieved a certain level of success, objective reflection offers you the opportunity to reassess your vision and goals in order to ensure that complacency does not set in.

Furthermore, this entire process is optimised if it is supported on a foundation of values that matter most to you and that ultimately align with your existing (or next) company. The values you live by, the reputation you acquire, the results you achieve, and how you interact with others and manage your own behaviours ultimately defines your personal brand reputation. As a process, this may seem quite simple to understand in theory; however, the reality is that over the course of your career lifetime it will be an ongoing challenge for you to uphold and implement.

Framing this process using the Career Pyramid Model (shown on the following page) may help you to visualise your way forward and ultimately guide you in your career journey.

Achievement & Reflection
Where to from here?

Actions
Measurable

Goals
Must be linked to your vision

Vision
Your definition of success

Self Awareness
Get to know yourself

Values

Personal Brand

Career Pyramid Model

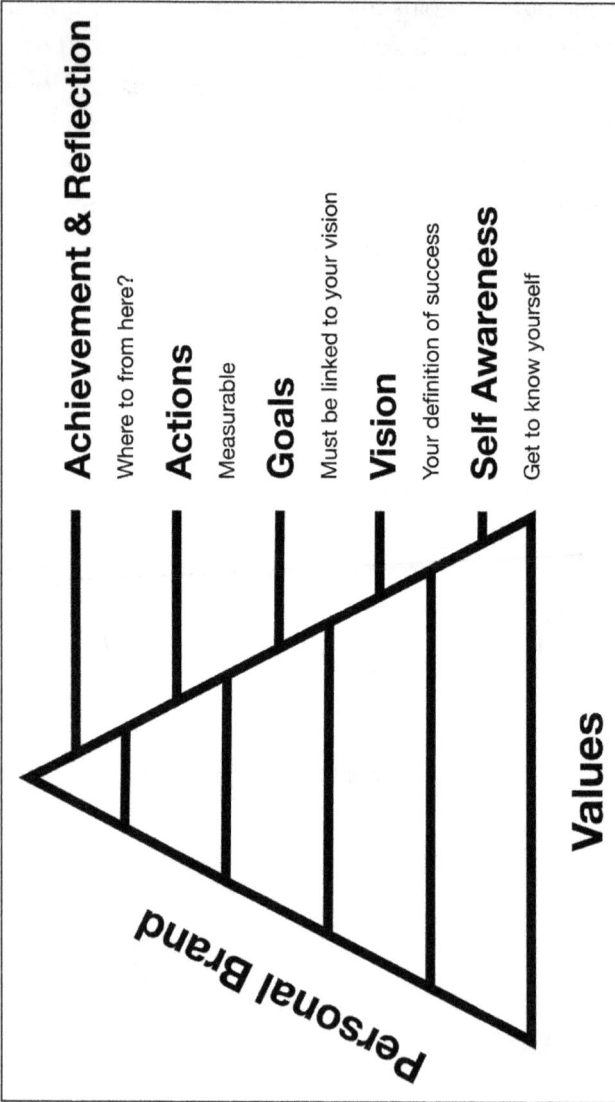

(Bruce Harkness 2018)

I sincerely hope this book has provided you with a degree of insight into modern workplaces and a framework that will better equip you not only to perform to your full potential in your work but also to enhance your enjoyment of your career and to help move you closer to your definition of success. My intention when writing this book was to structure it so that the content was easy to follow and apply, and could be read in one sitting or dipped into once you'd had sufficient time to reflect on each chapter. Most importantly, it is my hope that, in some small way, the content of this book will help to make your career journey just that little bit more satisfying.

During my own career and life so far, my path has crossed some of the most inspiring and interesting people I could ever hope to meet and I look forward to meeting many more in the future. Their own definitions of success varied according to what they valued most. However, what I have observed within the context of business is that *the difference between a true champion and a winner is not how often they win, it's what they do when they lose that defines them.*

So what will you do next after reading this book? We live in wonderfully exciting times with an abundance of choices and change. I hope you achieve your vision of success for your career and enjoy every step of your journey.

About the Author

Bruce Harkness has over 20 years' experience working in the fields of Human Resources, leadership and talent development. He has worked internationally in Europe, Middle East, Africa, Asia and United States of America, as well as in Australia, where he currently resides with his family.

Bruce has led large-scale change management initiatives in a number of multinational corporations, including Carlson Rezidor Hotel Group and Wyndham Vacation Resorts and Hotels: two of the world's largest hotel management companies. In addition, he has a passion for performance-focused business coaching.

Prior to his corporate career, Bruce took a very different path and throughout his school years he could have been best described as disruptive, having attended three different high schools due to unruly behaviour. Unwise choices in his early years saw him taking 'a road less travelled'.

Bruce also spent time in the Australian Army where he trained and served as an infantry officer. He went on to complete a Bachelor of Arts at Edith Cowan University and, some years later, he graduated with a Masters of Science in Organisational Coaching and Mentoring from Sheffield Hallam University in the United Kingdom.

On a personal level, Bruce is passionate about his family, the great outdoors and travel. Above all, he is a eternal optimist!

www.ingramcontent.com/pod-product-compliance
Lightning Source LLC
Chambersburg PA
CBHW060034210326
41520CB00009B/1128